MARTHA GRAHAM

Portrait of the Lady as an Artist

MARTHA GRAHAM

Portrait of the Lady as an Artist

Text by LeRoy Leatherman

Photographs by Martha Swope

NEW YORK | ALFRED A. KNOPF | 1966

FIRST EDITION

FOR BETHSABEE DE ROTHSCHILD

Author's Note:

Only those dancers who performed with Martha Graham during her season in November 1965 at the Broadway Theatre in New York City are written about in this text. Since Miss Swope's photographs were taken over a period of years, several former distinguished company members appear in them. They include Paul Taylor, Dan Wagoner, Richard Gain and Richard Kuch, Akiko Kanda and Miriam Cole.

MARTHA GRAHAM

Portrait of the Lady as an Artist

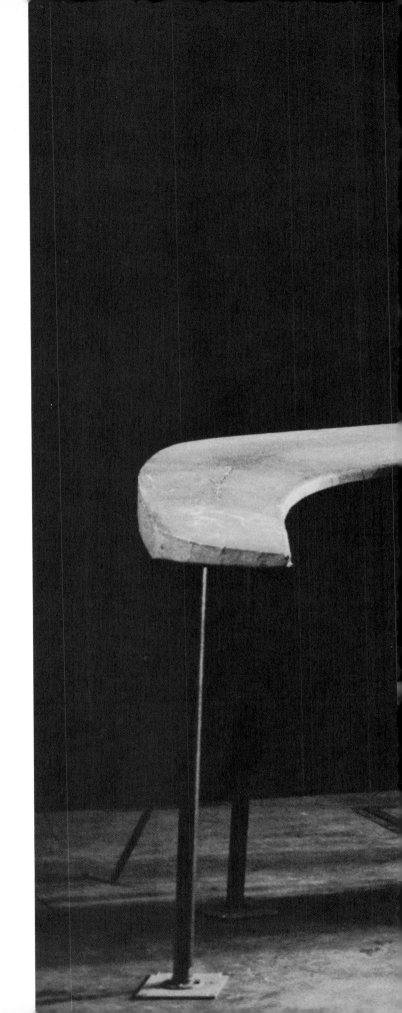

ACROBATS OF GOD

6

EMBATTLED GARDEN

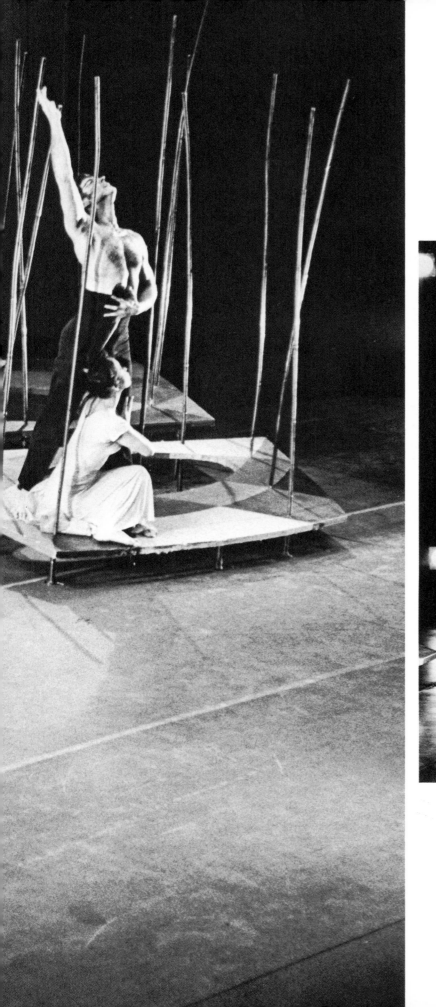

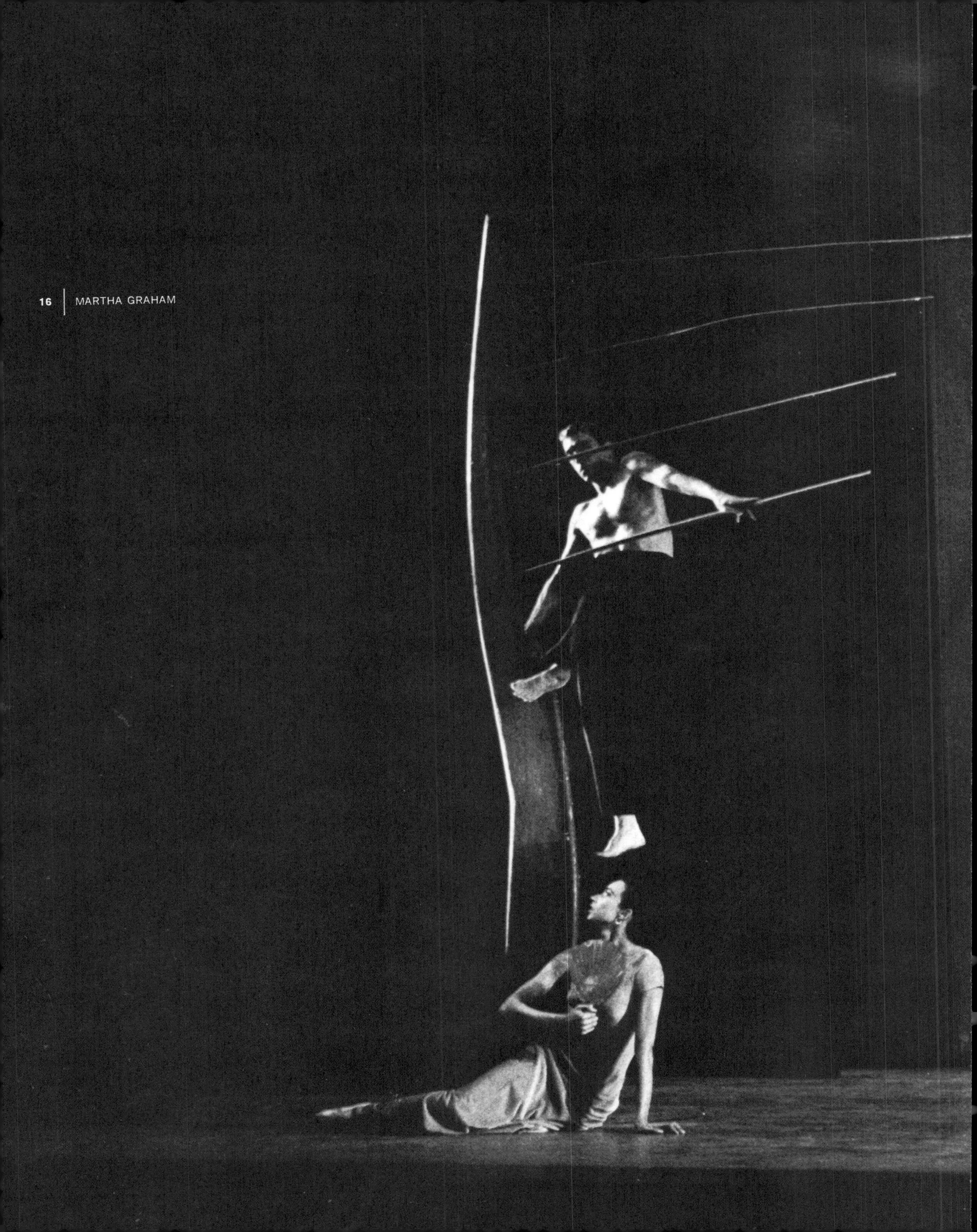

PART REAL—PART DREAM

In 1949, when she did a work about King Lear for her company and a twenty-five minute solo for herself about the Biblical Judith, performed in front of a full symphony orchestra, Martha Graham was also working on a comedy about Folly and the pursuit of it. She planned to use the aphorisms ("Do not be too much of a dove," for example) of Gracian, the mediaeval Spanish monk and she had cast herself in the part of Folly. At the end, having been pursued by a rich variety of fools, she was to ascend from the stage triumphant in an antique balloon. The music was composed by Paul Nordoff to her written script and delivered to her, but she never did *Folly,* not because she had too many other things on her mind, but no doubt, because she was not ready within herself, beyond the thinking stage, to deal with all the aspects of that vast subject. She chose one aspect, vanity, and used the music for a solo, *Gospel of Eve,* about a frivolous woman trying on hats. It was not successful and she dropped the subject and did not take it up again until 1960, when she was also working on the myth of Alcestis and was preoccupied with the thought of death. By then, she no longer saw herself as Folly, irresistible, eternally pursued and triumphant, but as foolish and she did a play called *Acrobats of God,* a title she took from her reading about the early Church fathers who, practising their austerities in the desert, came to be named *athletae dei. Acrobats* is high comedy and God has no role in it, except that it is about the art of dance and about the artist and for Martha, as for Our Lady's juggler, the deity is not only willing to be entertained but eager to be, acknowledging that the stretchings and strainings of the dancer and the austerities demanded of the artist are as worthy of honor as athletics of the soul performed in deserts by ascetics. The first statement Martha made about this new play to Carlos Surinach, whom she had chosen to compose the music for it, was uttered in her vibrant, low-pitched voice: "I want to describe dancers as the most beautiful things in all God's creation, but at the same time I want you to be silly about it."

She must have said much the same thing to Isamu Noguchi, for he designed for *Acrobats* a broad caricature of a dance studio and a choreographer's workshop. The indispensable barre is raised to a height impossible for any practical uses and distorted from a long pole, smoothed and polished by the sweat of dancers' hands, into a boomerang with a dangerously raked surface. The choreographer's chair or bench or whatever she might sit on while thinking is turned into a squat stool whose small round seat is inclined at about a forty-degree angle, so that she may at any moment slide off in a heap onto the floor. The indispensable mirrors are replaced by a free-form wooden slab, painted yellow, which hangs in front of the stool; only the choreographer may look into it, and on occasion, she hides behind it. The piano is replaced by three mandolinists who provide as required tinkly, twangy or sentimentally romantic comments upon the action. At curtain time, Martha and David Wood, who represents the dance company's indispensable régisseur, take their places stage center at the barre. For the role she plays, her costume is what she would call an "arrangement." A red-yellow-orange-gold strapless evening dress with a cumbersome train, it is a sari given to her by Rukmini Devi when she was in Madras. Revering it as a gift and as a garment, she refused to cut it and spent many hours at the mirror draping and redraping it about her before she fashioned it to suit herself. David Wood wears a black turtle-neck shirt and tight, brilliant red pants and carries an absurdly long whip.

The curtain rises, the orchestra blares and the scene is abruptly a circus. The régisseur becomes a whip-cracking ringmaster and he proceeds to handle the dancers, the acrobats, as if they are animals to be tamed, taught, and shown off doing tricks. He puts them through hazards and death-defying stunts—to the spectator who can detach himself from the play's development and concentrate strictly on what Martha and the company are doing physically on stage, her works often seem like obstacle courses designed by a fiend—for circus reasons, to delight, astonish, and bedazzle with the skill of it all, but also to parody the stunts themselves and to laugh at virtuosity practiced in art as an end in itself. Martha, the artist, takes little part in this: she observes, makes distant comments, and from time to time corrects an acrobat who is falling short of virtuosity; otherwise, most of the time, she keeps to herself. The ringmaster, presuming to bother her, finds her all but untamable. Viewed from the truest angle, Martha is in fact alone on the stage throughout *Acrobats.* What she has done in it for the first time in her long creative life is to take down the walls and allow anyone who wishes to look in upon her as she is when she works.

Acrobats is an incisive caricature of herself both as woman and as artist and, by immediate

29

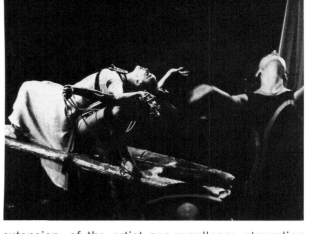

RIGHT: *Night Journey*
BELOW: *Acrobats of God*

extension, of the artist par excellence struggling through the initial phases of the creative process. The stage design exemplifies that state of mind when, inching toward the moment to begin to work, the artist takes the first look into himself and inevitably finds everything inside there crazily askew. The whip-cracking ringmaster is Martha, the part of her which drives the dancers to greater and greater mastery of their art and, much more difficult, drives and disciplines her and makes it possible for her to accomplish something. She is in the midst of defying her urge to creativity and her will when the play begins. When the dancers come leaping and flying across the stage, they appear as an arrogant display of the ideas and inspirations which she can easily summon up, easily make use of, she is saying to the stern disciplinary part of herself, if she only cared to, but she does not. She does not feel like it. She prefers to sit at her mirror and contemplate herself, the lone, unconquerable tigress in the gaudy evening gown. Yet she is doomed from the start to be tamed: simultaneous with the circus, there is the comical but bitter battle and she ends subdued, triumphant over nothing but herself, by no means in a mood to ascend, simply ready to get to work. The woman becomes a lady; the slothful vaporous creature becomes an artist, and the caricature becomes a candid handsome portrait in profile.

Virtually nothing has ever been said about the artist that does not apply to Martha; this is only another way of saying that she is more intensively and extensively human than the rest of us, and this is only another way of saying that with her at any moment the worst, short of out-and-out punishable crime, may be expected and certainly the best. Some who have had the experience describe working closely with her as something like living in a fragile tent high up on the slope of an active volcano (she herself hints at this in *Acrobats*), but it is much more like being fixed in outer space where meteors, fiery bolts, suns, and cool moons come flying by from all directions. Another kind of cosmos whose seasons and rotations, storms, breezes, and calm clear days Martha has complete charge of, it is a risky but wonderful place to be.

As a dancer; as the inventor of a technique of dance which has irrevocably changed the art; as a teacher; as a choreographer; as an actress whom many actors and exacting critics consider the greatest of her time; and, finally and most important, as a dramatist, Martha is unquestionably a genius. She is the first woman in the history of drama East and West to have contributed a huge and amazingly varied body of work to the theater. And not only that: she took over the stage as if nothing had ever happened on it before and created a new theater and a new kind of poetic drama.

She is a peculiarly American genius of whom Americans know very little. She and her company last toured America in 1949: since then, barring random, usually one-night-only appearances at the Hollywood Bowl or the Boston Arts Festival or the Connecticut College Dance Festival, they have performed exclusively on Broadway and on tours of Europe and the Middle and Far East, so there has been little opportunity for the public at large to see their art. Except for a collection of essays published in the early Thirties and long since out of print and a book of photographs by Barbara Morgan in 1941, next to nothing has appeared in print about Martha and her work outside of the dance press. Dance authorities and critics have written with fine perception and often movingly about her, but no one has attempted a full-scale study of her theater or a biography. There is good reason to believe no definitive biography ever will be written. An invaluable cache of source materials, every letter she had ever written to her mother, and she had written at least once a week from the time she first left home, Martha burned, for her own good reasons, when her mother died a few years ago. Louis Horst, the man who knew her best and longest, died recently and left no written reminiscences. Many of the living keep vivid memories of her (she never ambles through the memory, she streaks across it); a few have letters; there is a wealth of anecdotes, some amusing, some revelatory; there are the outward facts which make a record of little interest for Martha has kept strictly to herself, distant from events. She has spent her life working and is inseparable from her work. She is her own best subject; inner facts and inner events hold for her the true meaning of life. What she discovers when, as she would say, she "voyages" into herself, she puts directly onto the stage. The essential and meaningful things about her have always been on public view, for she has never hesitated to reveal herself in her art with an explicitness and candor most of us could not achieve in pitch darkness with a life-long lover. Because of this, a biographer must have seen all of her work, everything since 1926, and have grasped it thoroughly if he is to make sense out of her. Her work is by no means exclusively self-revelation: she has

taken many a cold hard look at the rest of us and at the world and made fine use of what she has seen, but she is by nature profoundly and ruthlessly introspective and, as an artist, safely so, for the world she voyages into has proved until now to be invariably human, common to all of us and evidently limitless.

Conflicting ancestral winds shaped some of the more jagged contours of that world. On the maternal side, her line has been traced back to Miles Standish. Her paternal great-grandfather, with some Black Irish blood in his veins, came to America from Scotland in steerage with Carnegie and Laughlin and made his fortune in Pittsburgh. Both branches of the family were rigidly Presbyterian. It happened, however, that Martha's father as a child with his brothers spent several years on his grandmother's antebellum plantation outside of Hannibal, Missouri. The boys were a wild lot, their grandmother saw the need of the ministry and herded them to services at the nearest available church, which was Roman Catholic. According to Martha, when her father was brought back home to Pittsburgh and confronted an austere Presbyterian service, he demanded to know what had happened to the music, the costumes, and the pomp. She feels that he never forgot nor ceased to be deeply influenced by the early exposure to ritual and to the *theater* of the Church and that at his death when she was a young girl he was in his heart a Roman Catholic. Her father's experience was duplicated in Martha's childhood, the Church substituted for by an illiterate Irish Catholic nurse named Lizzie, full of fantasies, fancies, and tales of worlds elsewhere, and just right for the tempestuous, imaginative child. Her mother, Presbyterian strictures notwithstanding, must have been fairly open-minded for later, when the child faced the problems of growing up—Martha says that she had a great many more of them than usual—she was permitted to talk about them with the parish priest. She suffered these early woes in Santa Barbara where, in addition to Lizzie and the priest, the splendor of Church ritual and the magnificence of the land and the Pacific, she also lived with an element of the Orient in the shape of Japanese and Chinese servants, gardeners, launderers, cooks which left its mark permanently upon her. Nevertheless, Presbyterianism and the stark New England view of things prevailed. From a novelist's point of view, it is a very satisfactory beginning; from Martha's, as a dramatist, it has served her splendidly. As a situation, it is a trap and, perhaps, uniquely American; no other country is likely to have provided such a variety of religious, moral, ethical and cultural strains and conflicts for a child to attempt to deal with. It is the artist's trap: the individual, unique in his time and place, seeking to realize himself in the midst of the abrasive tensions the past thrusts into the present. It is, in the long run, the human trap, never to be sprung, but open to investigation. Martha has recognized it and explored it as such. Its teeth are clamped on one's vital parts and in Martha's case the harder they bite the more powerful her work is.

She began to let the world know where the teeth were sharpest and the bite hurt most as early as April 18, 1926, at the Forty-Eighth Street Theatre in Manhattan, in her first performance as an independent creative artist. On that occasion, she did eighteen dances to the music of Franck, Schumann, Schubert, Brahms, Debussy, Scriabin, Ravel, Rachmaninoff, de Falla and others, which ranged in theme and atmosphere from *The Maid with the Flaxen Hair* and *Claire de Lune* to desire to a Tanagra figurine to *A Florentine Madonna* to Gopi Indian Maidens to a marionette show to a *Gypsy Portrait.* Later that year she did dances of rejoicing and contrition to Bloch's *Baal Shem;* to a score by Debussy, *The Moth,* with a program note which read, "The woman, like the white moth seeking the light, stalks the streets of Granada"; and *Three Poems of the East,* with the note, "She like a dancer puts her broidered garments on." Between 1926 and 1934, she danced about the First World War in *Poems of 1917;* about tragedy and comedy about petulance, remorse, politeness, and vivacity in *Four Insincerities;* about *Adolescence* and the *Heretic;* and about futility and ecstasy. She did a solo called *Lamentation* to make fully visible what it is like when one truly laments. She danced encased in a long tube of elastic purple cloth, demonstrating very early her unique ability to exploit theatrical costume as poetic metaphor. She danced about pessimism and optimism. She danced an "Ave" and a "Salve" in *Two Primitive Canticles* and the masterpiece *Primitive Mysteries* in three parts: *Hymn to the Virgin, Crucifixus* and *Hosanna.* In what she now refers to as her "long woolen period," she did *Dolorosa, Dithyrambic, Incantation, Offering, Elegies, Ekstasis, Tragic Patterns: Three Choric Dances for an Antique Greek Tragedy,* with choruses for Suppliants, Maenads and Furies, *Celebration* and *Integrals: Shapes of Ancestral Wonder.*

The extremes of Martha's temperament, the fixed magnets of her imagination, and the forces at work upon her, are there in the language, the old high words charged with history and formality, with the sense of ceremony and the ritualistic act and with the sense of God. The opposites clash: Catholic Rome, ancient Greece, Protestantism, the Orient; sin and contrition against the need for rejoicing and ecstasy; an intense and growing spirituality against an equally intense sensuality; the state of being a woman, virgin-lover-mother-lady-temptress-wanton all at the same time.

Suddenly, in 1934, she settled into her American dilemma and remained in it, except for a few significant voyages outside, for ten years. She did *American Provincials* in two parts, one about piety, the other about judgment; the renowned solo *Frontier: An American Perspective of the Plains,* in which for the first time she used stage decor; *Horizons,* about migration, new trails, dominion, "sanctified power," building, homesteading, and rejoicing; *American Lyric; American Document; Columbiad; El Penitente,* about a southwestern Indian flagellant sect, in which she again danced the Virgin; *Letter to the World* and *Salem Shore,* both an abrupt turn away from the broad vistas and rich visions of the American drive westward back to Protestant New England; *Every Soul is a Circus* and *Punch and the Judy,* both very American comedies; and finally *Appalachian Spring.*

Early in her career as a dancer, Martha was offered by a wealthy woman the opportunity to study with Mary Wigman in Germany; she declined, she says now, because she knew she had "something" and that she had to discover it and establish it in America, then she would go to Europe on her own. By 1934, she had discovered many facets of that "something" and had achieved, though she had not yet performed outside of America, as secure and far reaching a dominion over her art as had Picasso over painting, Stravinsky over music, Wright over architecture. But this period of discovery and achievement had brought her so far only to the eastward islands; like Columbus, she stood off the mainland, the American spirit in its poetic depths remained to be explored and it was through this exploration that the "something" emerged in full light and she became masterfully a dramatist. From her frontier she looked westward; never, interestingly enough, glancing to the rich, violent history and culture of the American South where some of her forbears had lived and endured the Civil War. As her titles suggest, her imagination was captured by the idea of new lands to be settled and cherished; by new powers and perspectives, and this was perhaps because in her voyage into herself she had come to a place as vast and unexplored as the West, the richness of whose resources freed her to come to grips with some of her old abiding conflicts. This she did in *Letter to the World*. This, her first play, was something entirely new in the history of the theater for in it for the first time——and it has not happened since——movement, poetry, and music, costumes, and decor were perfectly fused. Martha had not before this attempted to portray an historical figure, except for the mother of Christ; hindsight makes it inevitable that Emily Dickinson should have been the figure who first absorbed her. *Letter to the World* was a distillation in roughly fifty uninterrupted minutes of the life and art of Emily Dickinson and of a large portion of Martha herself. In it she finally confronted "the shapes of ancestral wonder," of Protestant New England doom, piety, judgment, everlasting death and damnation, and came to an understanding with them.

Two years later, in 1943, in an unforgettable voyage away from her American situation, she confronted other shapes less ancestral but no less immediately present and active in another region of herself. In *Deaths and Entrances* she made out of the highly charged lives of the Brontë sisters a play inexorable in its drive toward the brink of madness and Gothic in its resolution in a bolt of lightning and booming thunder. The story is told that on the night of the premier of this work at Bennington College, exactly when Martha, as Emily Brontë, rushed to the brink, real lightning struck and thunder boomed, as if she had summoned the elements. She may have; there is witchery in her and one would be unwise to doubt that certain dark powers are inaccessible to her.

She came back from the world of the Brontës gentled for the time and restated her *entente cordiale* with her ancestral shapes in *Appalachian Spring*, her last work about America and the American spirit. Located again as an artist in her native landscape she was capable now of bringing the forces of the past with her and subjecting them to subtle transformations. A doomful "Ancestress," archetype of the mothering but smothering past, had loomed over the action of *Letter to the World*, as had the ghost of Cotton Mather;

brought into the paradise of the Appalachian wilderness, the Ancestress became an archetype of the Pioneer Woman, rugged and necessarily stern but compassionate, and Mather's ghost became an itinerant preacher with his band of silly female converts. *Appalachian Spring* is a lyrical, highly complex poetic play, but on the surface it tells a simple story about a young pioneer and his joyous, tremulous bride on their wedding day. At the end, they are married, the preacher has delivered his hellfire-and-brimstone sermon, the stage darkens and all present kneel, heads bowed down under mortality and doom. But the young bride cannot keep her head bowed, she cannot stay on her knees, she is up softly dancing her joy. She tries to restrain herself, kneels, but at once she is up again, reverent but irrepressible, boldly asserting herself against the image of a god incapable of condoning love and happiness on earth. It is a lovely and very satisfying catharsis for the bride, the play and for Martha. Having achieved it, she was free to go voyaging wherever and as far as she wished.

Appalachian Spring was her one hundred and eighth work. By this time she was in complete charge of every element of her theater and nothing was seen or heard in it which had not come into being exclusively for it. She had stopped dancing to the music of the classical and early modern composers in 1930, choosing instead scores by Honegger, Krenek, Kodaly, Toch, Villa-Lobos, Bartok, Schoenberg, Hindemith, Chavez, Lopatnikoff, Varèse, and others. Louis Horst, who was the first to compose music for her, wrote many of her most important early works, including

Primitive Mysteries and *Frontier;* after 1934, she would use nothing, with very rare exceptions, but original music. When Aaron Copland wrote *Appalachian Spring* for her, she had already commissioned scores by Riegger, Antheil, Nordoff, Lloyd, Diamond, Cowell, North, Green and Johnson, establishing an artistic policy which has been followed, whenever possible, by all other modern dancers. She had reached a pinnacle and she might justifiably have rested there, but she is incapable of resting on any pinnacle. In those days, as now, as she searched for new composers, new sculptors and designers for her stage decor, she was reading insatiably, moving farther and farther away from her early influences. Zen Buddhism, the philosophies of India, the writings of Carl Jung and his followers; poetry, ancient and modern, from Sappho and the Haiku to Eliot, Robert Lowell, St. John Perse and Dylan Thomas, from one of whose poems she took the title *Deaths and Entrances;* classical Greece, the art and drama of Japan, Etruscan, Chinese, and Middle Eastern art; the world of myths, legends, and fairy tales—all have continued to fascinate her and to feed her imagination. Since 1944, finding her inspiration in an astonishing variety of sources, she has created for herself and her company more than twenty-five plays. Some were unsuccessful and had few performances. Some were minor. Most rank with her major earlier achievements and some outrank them. All, whether failures or successes, have proved that she continues to be, as she always has been, incapable of the superficiality, banality, vulgarity and cynicism of her time. She has never, as she says, been interested in

anything small. She knows despair, but not the existential kind. Nihilism is incomprehensible to her. She has kept her head throughout this dizzying century and for nearly forty years her theater has been one of the few places in the Western world where one could be certain to find impeccable taste, a vaulting ambition and, no matter what the subject, an affirmation of man. Her art insists upon human individuality and responsibility, upon the meaningfulness of human experience, even the darkest, and upon the immediate possibility of what Joseph Conrad's Marlowe, struggling to define courage, summed up as:

> *. . . that inborn ability to look temptations in the face—a readiness unintellectual enough, goodness knows, but without pose—a power of resistance, don't you see, ungracious if you like but priceless—an unthinking and blessed stiffness before the outward and inward terrors, before the might of nature and the seductive corruption of men—backed by a faith invulnerable to the strength of facts, to the contagion of example, to the solicitation of ideas.*

The resistance, the stiffness, the faith characterize Martha herself and give her plays and their protagonists, particularly those she enacts, much of their power and radiance.

Varied as her recent sources have been, her titles and themes continue to be redolent of the persistent sentiments of her existence. *Diversion of Angels,* lyrical and joyous in the mood of the bride in *Appalachian Spring,* is about youth and the delights and occasional pains of being in love for the first time. *Embattled Garden* goes a step

Seraphic Dialogue

farther, from innocence to knowledge. Wry, satirical, it is ostensibly about Adam and Eve, Lilith, Adam's first and very knowing wife, and the serpent turned into The Stranger. The atmosphere is, however, distinctly Spanish, Eden is a thicket of green poles stuck in a garish ground and Adam and Eve seem less to live in it than to be trapped there, like any lovers trapped in the time when passion has lapsed and love is in such question that it needs a jolt. The Stranger lives up in a gaunt tree and when the curtain rises Lilith sits below him mechanically fanning as Eve in the thicket listlessly combs her hair. It is a hot torpid day when the weather seems to mock the dead weight on the spirit of *la vie quotidienne* and any intruders into the garden are welcome, no matter what their mischief. From his tree The Stranger leaps into the torpor and some lively mischief follows, all in the cause of change, to break the monotony of virtue, but Adam vanquishes The Stranger, he and Eve reaffirm their past if not their present love and return to their thicket, and Eve combs her hair as The Stranger goes back up in his tree and Lilith again sits fanning. It will all happen again, but nothing will change, except that the lovers in their excursions outside the garden of romantic love will gather day by day more and more to forgive each other for.

Seraphic Dialogue, about Joan of Arc, is Martha's spiritual testament, her declaration that, paradoxically, it is only through one's willingness to be the instrument of higher powers that one achieves individuality and wholeness. Exalted, ecstatic, in the tradition of the visionary saints, it is the most beautiful of all her works and, without being in the least sectarian, it is probably the great religious play produced in this century. *A Look at Lightning* was about, among other things, the poet's encounters with the errant muse. *Canticle for Innocent Comedians* (unfortunately no longer in the repertory, for in it Martha showed her full capabilities as a theatrical magician), was a celebration in the spirit of Saint Francis of Assisi of the beauty and wonder of the natural world. *Legend of Judith* is a testament of loneliness and despair, a confrontation with the emptiness of glory and with the price one may pay for having been the willing instrument. In an early version of this play before it reached the stage, the curtain was to come down as Martha, playing the aged Judith, turned her back on the audience for the first time in her life and walked away into the dark. Now, when the curtain falls, she stands on a kind of promontory alone, facing the audience, but with her face veiled.

Ranging widely through her European heritage, she did plays inspired by Mallarmé's *Herodiade,* by Shakespeare's *Lear (Eye of Anguish)* and *Antony and Cleopatra (One More Gaudy Night)*, and by Milton's *Samson Agonistes.* In *Episodes* she dealt with Mary, Queen of Scots. *Ardent Song* was about three goddesses, Aphrodite, Hecate and Aurora, and their powers over men. *Dark Meadow* had no identifiable sources and Martha says she still does not know what it meant. Her most abstruse but among her most powerful works, it seemed to take place in the most primitive and elemental region of the psyche where an archetypal rite of the seasonal cycle and of the cycle of death, mourning and rebirth was enacted.

Episodes: Part I: Martha Graham as Mary, Queen of Scots

In 1946, however, she began to find in Greek mythology the primary myths of her own being and experience. She has used Medea in *Cave of the Heart,* the Minotaur in *Errand Into the Maze,* Oedipus and Jocasta in *Night Journey,* Clytemnestra, Alcestis, Phaedra and Circe to create modern equivalents in depth and purity of intent to the dramas of classical Greece. Her concept of drama and of the function of theater has always been, in fact, essentially Greek: entertain, delight though the play may and must, it must also, if it is to have any value, be good for the soul, and must move, purge and elevate the spirit. For the spectator who fully participates, her plays are ritualistic experiences.

She used the story of Medea to show how evil works and how it looks when it is triumphant. In *Errand Into the Maze* she replaced Theseus with a woman, herself, and added a new dimension to the myth by making the Minotaur the prefiguration of fear itself and, simultaneously, fear's object, so that the two were inseparable. She cast an entirely new light into the depths of the Oedipus myth by making Jocasta the protagonist of *Night Journey;* the quintessence of womanhood and of queenliness, Jocasta is one of her finest achievements and the play itself, while encompassing all of the essential elements of the tragedy and positing thereby the existence of an incomprehensible and malign Fate, is an intense declaration of love. *Alcestis* is an equally intense declaration of faith: led to this myth by her preoccupation with the thought of death, she made a play that is an affirmation of life and of the inevitability of spring. *Phaedra,* that *cause célèbre,*

is of course about lust, lust as evil, one of the seven deadly sins and, perhaps, in Martha's view, the deadliest, for it is the one most likely utterly to dehumanize. The play is straightforwardly erotic; the question is whether it is excessively so, and the answer may have been given by a spectator who, getting out into the fresh air when the curtain fell, said he thought he would not seek any carnal adventures for at least a couple of weeks.

Clytemnestra, which covers the essentials of the *Oresteia* as well as certain signal events of the *Iliad,* is the summation of Martha's artistry. According to one critic, it stands in the history of drama where Joyce's *Ulysses* stands in the history of the novel: it is as bold an experiment, as radical a departure. It is entirely unlike anything she had ever done before except that, as her imagination drives through the passions and violence of the myth, her theme is again redemption—the self-redemption of Clytemnestra, the queen who ruled like a man, wife and murderess of Agamemnon, wanton mistress of Aegisthus, adoring mother of Iphigenia, loathing and vengeful mother of Electra and Orestes, a woman who would seem to be beyond redemption, but Martha manages it close to the last minute of the action at a single stroke, with a single act of love.

In November, 1965, at the 54th Street Theatre in Manhattan, she presented, in addition to the current repertory, two new works, *The Witch of Endor* and *Part Real—Part Dream,* and revivals or, better, restorations, danced by the younger stars of the company, of *Primitive Mysteries, Appalachian Spring,* and *Cave of the Heart.* The months preceding this engagement were a time of "black despair" for her. Waking each morning, she could see no reason "to get up and go through the day." Love of life and of the world and its creatures had sustained her all her years; it pervades everything she had done in the past and it is the *raison d'être* of even her darkest works. She seemed to have lost it. Her unforgettable laughter was not to be heard. Her smiles were rare and wan. No one had ever seen her in such a state and everyone knew that the throes of creativity could not be blamed for it. Inaccessible, self-destructive, she dragged herself through the days and nights of work. Her doctors were gravely concerned, for her health and her legendary stamina seemed to be failing; one of them was convinced that the attempt she was making to bring herself and her company back to the stage was a deliberate courtship with death. Yet there is not the slightest indication of this woeful state of affairs in *Part Real—Part Dream.* It is the work of a teller of fairy tales, an enchantress ranging through the "holy jungle of the imagination," where, she says, the action takes place, with no other purpose than to quicken and delight. For three or four years she had been talking about doing a "kind of fairy tale" and she was going to play the witch, "not, of course, the ordinary kind of witch," but she changed her mind, did the play for her company and cast herself as the Witch of Endor in a very different kind of play. There are clear indications in it of her deeply troubled state and of what caused it. *The Witch of Endor* has affinities, in the bleakness of its atmosphere and in its questioning of the fruits of action, with *Legend of Judith.* Like *Samson Agonistes* it is a deliberate attempt on Martha's part to create a tragedy in which the protagonist is played by someone other than herself, thus to shift the focus away from herself, to accept her dispensability as an actress on her stage and yet for a while to remain there. Like *Samson Agonistes,* it is not yet a successful attempt, but it is much more promising in that its theme is about what is behind the attempt itself: the loss of power which comes with age, the displacement of old heroes by the young, the fact that the time comes when even the greatest can see no place to go but down.

By the last week of October, 1965, the normal tensions that go with the approach to an opening night in the theater were so heightened by apprehension about Martha that the atmosphere at the 54th Street Theatre was all but insupportable. In rehearsals on stage she was like someone back from the dead. She performed her usual miracles of work, as everyone has long since taken for granted, but she did them listlessly. The essential Martha was absent, perhaps forever. But Martha lives her legend with unfailing virtuosity: once she had gotten through opening night, she returned, and for three weeks, the longest time she had ever appeared on Broadway, she and the company brilliantly performed the largest repertory they had ever offered in what turned out to be the most successful engagement in their history.

Having taken down the walls and revealed and spoofed herself in *Acrobats of God,* Martha may be seen to have meant to reveal from another angle something else: how, practically speaking, this repertory came into being; how, specifically, she works; how she and her company work together and on what basis. During the last minutes of *Acrobats,* while the artist, with hard-won stature, slowly paces back and forth along the absurd barre, followed by the disciplinary part of herself which has prevailed, the dancers come singly onto the stage, bow to her and stand with their backs to the audience, as if in position to begin a class. There is a breath in the music, Martha stops for a split second, stands as ready as they, then bows to them—but also across them and through them to the disciplinary ringmaster. The final movement, a quick turn and bow to the audience, is like an afterthought. With these bows that she and her dancers make to each other, they sum the matter up. Beyond all the quibbles and squabbles and fights, the loves and flirtations, jealousies and rivalries, troubles real and imaginary, and the genuine pain that are inevitable when fine-strung human beings work together toward a work of art; beyond all this which is the raw material of *Acrobats,* the truth for Martha and the company lies in the high dignity and respect of the formal bow. Their whole remarkable world rests squarely upon the import of it.

Their place of work, officially called the Martha Graham School of Contemporary Dance, now incorporated as a tax-exempt educational institution, was for many years a cramped studio at 66 Fifth Avenue in Manhattan. There Martha, alone at first, afterward with members of her growing company, taught the technique of dance she invented and trained many of the major and minor choreographers and performers of the thirties and forties, many actors and actresses, innumerable teachers and hordes of others who simply enjoyed the work. Since 1952, the School has been located in a three-story red brick building, with dishevelled gardens on both sides, at 316 East 63rd Street and at this site is has become increasingly what it was from the beginning: interprofessional (actors, housewives, secretaries, young businessmen, a Marine or two, a minister or two, etc., all mixed in with the serious dancers), interracial and international. In any given class, among the sundry Americans of all colors, creeds and backgrounds, there may be students from India, Korea, Thailand, Japan, England, France, Germany, and the Scandinavian countries, from Central and South America, New Zealand, Greece, and Israel (by the score), many of whom arrive and manage well without being able to speak English, most of whom have come to America expressly to study at the Graham School.

They are taught what Agnes de Mille once described as "an original way of communication . . . a new system of leverage, balance and dynamics . . . a code of technique which constitutes the most beautiful sustained movement by a living composer." It is all of this and in this order of significance: from the beginning of her career as a creative artist, Martha aimed for the theater, for ways of moving that would communicate varieties of human experience which the art of dance had never before attempted to communicate, and ultimately for dramas that would be acted through movement alone.

As a teacher, Martha is uncompromising and with a student who is not, as she would say, a realist, she may be ruthless: "A dancer must be a realist. The toe is pointed or it is not. You are in competition with no one but yourself. Do the work as it should be done or get out and never come back." She tells her students that the technique is a medium for "the cultivation of the body"; therefore, their task is not to learn to execute a series of exercises with maximum grace but the much more difficult one of perfecting an instrument capable of responding to any artistic demands made upon it. The demands she will make are dramatic. The technique as taught is devoid of verbal content; no movement or series of movements has meaning. Communication occurs when the technique, once mastered, is put to use in the dramatic situation and there every movement must be meaningful. Martha hammers away at this, never allowing the student to forget that what he is in fact attempting to learn is a technique of *acting* and that he is aspiring to a place not in a dance but in a play. Then, for her, it becomes a question of *who* is acting and *what* is being truthfully acted. That the technique is a medium for the cultivation of the body is not enough: it is also, and more important, a medium for the "cultivation of the being." Beginners are bewildered by this pronouncement. Few, if any, arrive having given much thought to the cultivation of their being; they are not accustomed to such talk and they could not be prepared for such a spiritual attitude toward dance. Martha's tone of voice, her formidable presence, radiant or rampaging, may rivet and enchant them, but for a long time they do not understand what she is talking about and some go away thinking she does not know herself. Those who stay and work hard long enough, even those who have no ambition to be dancers, eventually learn that she does know and find that, by some means they

could never define, they have changed as individuals.

This conception of her art has its roots far back in Martha's childhood. Her first dance lesson, she says, was taught to her by her father. A graduate of Johns Hopkins, he was a general practitioner; for a number of years he practiced at a mental institution near Pittsburgh and he kept throughout his life a deep interest in nervous and mental diseases. One day, when he was a very small child, he caught her telling him a lie. She could not understand how he knew and demanded an explanation. He told her it was the way she had moved as she spoke and that he had learned from his patients to take as heavily into account the way they moved as what they said, for movement never lied. A simple lesson, deceptively so; it stuck tight in her mind and worked on her, sharpening her eye to the differences between what people said and how they moved. More often than not, it was as though they were strangers to their bodies, like nonbelievers in houses of worship. When she had become a dancer and was earning her living by performing, first with the Denishawn Company, then in the Greenwich Village Follies, the lesson must have worked increasingly against her, an inner voice insisting that the matter was not so simple and that as a dancer, if she were not precisely lying, she could not either be said to be telling the truth. Once, for example, with the Denishawn Company, she had appeared as a Japanese house-boy, assisting Miss St. Denis in a dance about flower arranging. Her convincing performance led to a plan to turn her into a Japanese boy who was to be billed as a great Denishawn discovery. Her protest about what would happen when her breasts were fully developed was brushed aside: she would simply be bound up. Her mother learned of the plan and said no and saved her from an ambiguous early career.

(The Denishawns had extra-artistic uses as well to put her to. There is now an Alice-Through-The-Looking-Glass fantasy about the very notion, but they did once make her the bookkeeper for one of their tours and the ledger she kept still exists, with her meticulous and probably accurate entries in a handwriting already bold and authoritative. On another occasion, too busy to go themselves, she was sent to Los Angeles to negotiate a contract with Pantages, whose vaudeville circuit they were about to tour. Mr. Pantages was quite vulnerable to beautiful young women, the business side of the meeting was evidently quickly settled, and he asked Martha to go for a ride with him along the ocean. She replied, cryptically, "I'm going to the top, Mr. Pantages, and I'm not taking anybody with me." He replied graciously that if she ever needed help, money, anything, all she need do was to call on him any hour of the day or night. Though there were many times later when she needed help, money, everything, she never took advantage of his offer.)

Eventually with the Denishawns, she rose to a starring role as an Aztec princess. In the Follies she danced tangos in opulent Spanish-Moorish settings. She was an East Indian princess in a perfumed garden in the mood of "Pale Hands I Love Beside the Shalimar." She did an Apache number with Charles Weidman set in a Montmarte dive in the center of which loomed a black cauldron full of devils. She was very successful and recognized, young as she was, as a performer of unique power. She was very well paid. She had the expensive tastes she still has and indulged them. There is an indication that she moved in lively circles around town after the show. For a time she "chaperoned," she says, a dancer who shared her Follies dressing room on dates with Larry Fay, the gangster, traveling between the stagedoor and the speakeasies in his bullet-proof limousine. Withal, she was staunchly self-respectful and certain of the honor that is a dancer's due: once she was hired to dance at a party in a Long Island mansion, but she was instructed to arrive and depart by the servant's entrance; she announced that she would arrive with the guests at the front door and leave the same way and so she did.

Independent to her core, sensibly arrogant, single-mindedly ambitious, invulnerable, touchy as a tiger to handle: she was all of this in her early twenties, but something more, something essential. Abruptly, she left the Follies, left the money, relinquished (for the time being) her expensive tastes, left New York City. At last, consciously or unconsciously, she must have been seized by the full import of her father's lesson. It was not only that movement never lied; not only that this fact revealed a division in the brain between the part of it which uses words to say what one wants heard and the other part which directs motor responses; it was finally that, in the whole person, the *being,* there was something that insisted at all times on the truth, something that was, if not, so to speak, on the side of God, at least on the side of the better and the best, and this *something* used move-

ment—the bat of an eye, a twitch, an awkward posture, hands in the wrong place, head at the wrong tilt—to tell the truth, to reveal the individual and the state of his being on the instant.

She went to the Eastman School in Rochester to teach. Rouben Mamoulian, who hired her, says that she came upon the scene "like John the Baptist." Louis Horst was with her. He had played the piano in the pit when she appeared on a stage the first time. Considerably older than she, he had become in the years since then a great many things to her as a woman and as a dancer. For her as an artist, he was until 1949 the most important influence in her life. His contribution to her development is inestimable. He was her accompanist and musical director; he composed the first original scores she danced to and sought out among modern composers those who were right for her. Something of a quiet genius himself, and, finally, a unique figure in the history of modern dance, he seems to have had from the beginning a profound insight into Martha's genius and he was able to assist in its natural growth, acting as guide and mentor, driving her, slapping her hard when she needed to be slapped, helping her to drive herself into being what she was bound to be. Theirs was a highly charged, delicately balanced relationship, and it went through a number of phases, tumultuous and otherwise; each taught and was richly taught by the other for more than thirty years.

In Rochester in 1925, far enough away from Broadway, she taught dance and stage movement for actors and she worked with Louis's help on herself and with herself, cultivating that part of her being which insisted on the truth and cultivating her body to move in radically different ways and in radically difference contexts from those any dancer had ever attempted before. No airy flights, no willowy arms, no butterfly toes: she was not interested in beguiling the king and his court or anyone else into an untroubled fairy land. She meant to go straight into trouble of all human kinds and she needed for that a technique of movement which affirmed plain human facts and which was broad enough in scope and precise enough in its specific details to convey at any moment what anyone might feel. She did not set out to invent a dance language in the sense that, for example, the classical court dances of the Orient are essentially languages, each movement serving as a sign with an accepted literal meaning. Neither did she invent another style of mime, for mime relies for its effect upon the fact that, however broadened, the movements are familiar. In the long run, she did not even concentrate on dance as such for, in both the Eastern and Western traditions of the art up to her time, the spectator's pleasure derived not at all from the tale being told but from the skill and grace with which the movements were executed. No one goes to a Graham performance to see how well the dancers dance the steps; that is not the point for them nor for the audience. One goes to be moved and illuminated, to experience something of the truth of human existence and one knows that this will be accomplished through "an original way of communication."

How she achieved this way is one of the mysteries, but her approach to it is plainly visible in the technique itself. Many of its basic elements are centered in the pelvic and genital regions, and

Martha's bluntness in teaching them shocks the innocent. It is Renoir's bluntness when, asked by some fool how he achieved the lovely flesh tones of his canvases, he replied with the manifesto, "I paint with my penis." Reason, logic, the cautious brain have, in short, little to do with the creative process; the biological organism and the generative, procreative force have everything to do with it. Martha and Renoir would have agreed. Spiritual, mystical being though she is, and already was in Rochester, she has no patience with anyone who is not also natural. To her, virginity past a certain age is a most unnatural and unhealthy state, especially for an artist. She started and her art starts with basic facts, on the ground; the floor, equivalent to the hard, resistant but cultivable earth is her element as surely as the ballet dancer's element is clear empty air.

Having found her element and her way, she and Louis returned to New York City and spent a year preparing that single historic performance at the 48th Street Theatre. (Her choice of a legitimate Broadway theater as the place where she would first appear as an artist in her own right reveals her confidence and her daring, but it served also to elevate the whole of modern dance in the eyes of the public. This was not to be another "Dance Recital" or "Dance Concert"; it was something new, it had a different status and Broadway was its proper place. Succeed or fail, she was determined from the beginning, she says "to compete at the top.") Since then, she has never ceased to experiment with the technique, developing and enriching it according to the demands each new drama makes upon it. It has proved to be inex-

haustibly adaptable and, as a system, anatomically, absolutely sound. Properly taught and properly mastered, it moulds and strengthens the body without overdeveloping any part of the muscular structure, and it makes possible astonishing physical feats. The Graham dancers seem to have been sculptured in the classical Greek style. A Graham performance is a revelation of what the human body is capable of doing, and doing safely. Accidents and injuries are rather more the rule than the exception in most dance companies; they are all but unheard of in the Graham company and in the School.

For months during the hours between classes the School is as quiet as any other once the students have gone home. The teachers go to other jobs at the Neighborhood Playhouse School of the Theatre, where the technique and stage movement based upon it have been taught by Martha and the company members for twenty-five years or more to, among a great many others, Gregory Peck, Tony Randall, Eli Wallach, Richard Boone, Efrem Zimbalist, Jr., Anne Jackson, and Tammy Grimes; at the Juilliard School of Music which, since the early fifties, has offered the technique as part of its curriculum; at other institutions along the Eastern seaboard. Now some go regularly to teach in London, Stockholm, Jerusalem and Tel Aviv, and Mexico City. They go to work on their own choreography or with other choreographers; to rehearse for television appearances and on- and off-Broadway shows; or they go home to do the housekeeping and take care of the children. Martha may show up in these quiet times and she may not. She may be in her apartment reading, seemingly hap-

hazardly, taking notes and copying quotations in a shorthand notebook. She may be in a taxi going to Doubleday's to buy more books, seemingly at random, or to Bergdorf's to buy whatever, or to the mid-town fabric houses to look at costume materials. She may be anywhere, but she is working. The stillness is deceptive. The center of things is shifting.

There must be as many ways to undergo the creative process as there are individuals capable and willing to undergo it. In a sense, Martha is always in the midst of it, for there is a part of her that is avid, insatiable, incessantly writhing toward something new and she is quietly miserable until she comes upon it and it takes hold of her. Once it does, despite her immediate clarity as she meets those around her, it is as if she has been caught up by some huge bird full of spirit which at any instant may find her unsavoury and deposit her on a high inaccessible ledge or drop her into unmarked country. Each new work is the first work she has ever done and no amount of past accomplishment offers present security or comfort. She is pessimistic: "I've got the inspiration of a gnat." She despairs. Everyone who watches from below feels pessimistic with her and despairs. All she seems able to do is to hold onto a certain will to survive and a certain rusty discipline, but the flight is erratic, the grip loose, the will weak, the discipline nearly worn through. She has ended up on ledges before; she has been dropped. One forgets, as she does, that most of the time she has conquered the bird.

In this first phase, which Richard Wagner called the phase of "theoretical meditation," Mar-

tha is chary with news. If she speaks at any length about the new work, it usually means that she is trying to clear her mind for the real, as-yet-unspoken thing. Sometimes she hints. She may telephone to read something she has come across and it may be no more than a sentence or a captivating phrase like *athletae Dei* or "secular games" or "the holy jungle of the imagination." She may say she has been "brooding" for a long time about Phaedra or Lilith. The hints once dropped may never be mentioned again. Everyone waits as she searches among the innumerable possibilities until the single right one among them seizes her. There is of course no explanation of why only one among them does this, but when the work is on the stage it is possible to guess. She is driven to undertake those voyages into herself by the "something" in her being which insists upon the truth about her immediate situation. She speaks rarely about her personal crises because, no doubt, she plans to use them, suffer the voyage through them, then search for the plot and characters to embody them and resolve them by revealing them in a dramatic form which constitutes the truth. Given her state of mind in 1960, for example, *Alcestis* was a logical vehicle. But she did *Acrobats of God* at the same time. The flight of the bird, the course of her voyage is totally unpredictable and guessing later at explanations is a waste of time. The sure things are the phases of her work: when she begins to stay at home "to work on my script," it is certain that her theoretical meditations are over, and everyone feels the first optimism when she reports that she has chosen a composer and has sent him her new script.

Few but the composer ever see the work in this first form. She types the script herself by a rapid hunt-and-peck system from her notes, seldom makes a copy. Strictly speaking, it is not a script. It indicates the plot development in broad outline by specifying a sequence of dances, solos, duets, groups, each to last a certain number of minutes, each to convey through movement a certain phase of the action, and these are linked by poetic statements of her own, reflections, musings, and with quotations from her reading. Sometimes, perhaps more often than not, the sequence of dances is left out and all the composer gets is her poetic statements and the quotations, but they have their inner logic and usually suffice. Whatever its shape, the script is deliberately open and evocative. It allows the composer maximum freedom to work within the given theme and it reserves for Martha the freedom to take maximum advantage of his inspiration and to stick to or depart from her first thoughts as she wishes. At bottom, her scripts are written on the assumption that the composer as artist will be as responsive as she to what has captured her and in effect the script establishes between her and the composer a space in which the drama may freely grow.

She may not have originated this artistic method and this approach to the theater, but she has certainly perfected it and she has done most of her finest plays by following it. However, much militates against it and she has been forced to keep a remarkable resiliency in her working methods. There are times when there is no money to pay for a new score or when there is no time to wait for one to be written. On occasion, Martha has not been able to produce a script. In 1962, when she was asked to do a new work for the Connecticut College Dance Festival, there was no money and little time, but she had the phrase "secular games" on her mind and Robert Starer had a composition for small orchestra which he thought might do: *Secular Games,* a witty, light-hearted, charming work for the company was the result. When she agreed to do *Episodes* with the New York City Ballet, George Balanchine selected the two earliest scores of Anton Webern for her to work with and she did a play about Mary, Queen of Scots—she had been brooding about her for some time—and set up between her own art and her own relations with music and those of Mr. Balanchine a high gritty tension. Forced to adapt herself to a given set of conditions, or, as she would say, "to accept the inevitable," it is possible that she may be successful any time, so long as she has lived with her theme long enough. The deep process, if it is there and vibrant, may take advantage of what offers. If

it is not there or not yet ready, then time must tell. In 1953, when Martha needed a new work for herself for her Broadway season, she had no money, no time, and no script. William Schuman gave her one of his recent compositions and she did *Voyage.* Isamu Noguchi designed a setting which suggested the spare essentials of an expensive cruise: a ship's prow, gold-leafed, and a kind of sail that is also a cloud, all solid but all curiously insubstantial. The action concerned a woman and three men emotionally entangled. Martha wore a black evening dress she had bought from Hattie Carnegie some years before and the men wore dinner clothes in soft off-beat shades. The stage was beautiful but the play did not come off. If Martha had edged just slightly over into a different humor, it would have been high comedy; it kept threatening to be. She revised and recostumed it in 1955 and changed the title to *Theatre for a Voyage.* The four characters wore shades of red; still, it did not work. By 1963, she was working on the myth of Circe, she had commissioned a score from Alan Hovhaness, but now needed a set. She got out the ship's prow and the sail, saved some of her original ideas from *Voyage,* and gave the work, choreographed for the company, its premiere in London. Its mood is archaic, its impulse erotic, its atmosphere exotic, but it is perhaps what she had been aiming for all along. The woman in the Hattie Carnegie dress, the woman in red, had probably always been Circe.

In addition to their usefulness to the composer and their value as a record of how Martha's imagination works, her scripts show that as early as this, long before what is for her the "writing stage," she has solved one of the writer's major problems: structure. Here her sense of time directs her almost unerringly and it has dictated her innovations in dramatic structure. It is Joyce's in *Finnegan's Wake*—like *Embattled Garden,* a number of her works, circling back upon themselves, have ended precisely as they began—and William Faulkner's: "The past is not dead; it is not even past." For her as for them and for many contemporary thinkers, measured time is of little or no consequence. It is inner time that is significant. Today is not the sum of all our yesterdays, but of a few decisive days or hours or instants, and these are not lodged in the memory to be looked back upon, but are still being lived and are still directing our behavior in the here and now. Martha strikes into the action and into the lives of her characters at the critical instant when they become fully aware of this fact; when, in the midst of an immediate crisis, the seeming distinction between past and present is wiped out and understanding and reconciliation with reality become possible. Often, the known action of her plays is over when the curtain rises. When *Night Journey* begins, Jocasta is alone in her chamber swaying below a coiled rope she holds high; what happens afterwards is a single, long but instantaneous plunge through annihilating knowledge to death. Though Jocasta experienced the tragedy as news, as fact, in the full light of day, she does not live it until the last instant of her life.

Martha's original *Judith,* the solo, had a simple narrative structure built upon the night when the young chaste widow of Manasse, in order to save her people, transformed herself into the seductress and murderess of Holofernes. The later *Legend of Judith* has an aged heroine who is, despite the honor the world pays her, bereft. Her being turns still upon that night of transformation and of self-discovery which doomed her to glory and to a double widowhood. In this turning, this fine spinning of her soul upon the decisive point of its experience, she is attended by three angels and they precipitate a crisis during which she sees herself as she was—as she still is—as a bride and sees her bridegroom Manasse as he was, but, with the developing crisis, Manasse and Holofernes become the same man and in a stunning vision, a richly ambiguous dramatic metaphor, the aged Judith and the young Judith become entwined with him in a kind of totem made by the angels' wings. Their heads, their arms, their bodies, appear, disappear, alternate positions in a nightmare of identity, and when the totem dissolves, the aged Judith, not the young, seduces, loves, murders Holofernes again. She is all she ever was and discovered herself to be. What happened goes on happening.

The solo *The Triumph of Saint Joan* had, like the early *Judith,* a simple narrative structure built upon the stages of transformation from Joan as maiden to warrior to martyr. In adapting the work for her company, Martha kept those three figures and added a fourth, the immediate Joan as protagonist, and she developed the action out of the moment of Joan's apotheosis. *Seraphic Dialogue* is a set of watchful dialogues between Joan and the three phases of her legend and, despite the angelic presences which attend, her apotheosis is brought about by her own effort to understand.

Martha chose to start her version of the *Oresteia* near the end: Clytemnestra is already in the Underworld, fully as violent and vengeful as she was on earth, demanding to know of King Hades why she alone must go dishonored among the shades. This radical beginning led Martha into her farthest-reaching experiment with dramatic structure and the suspension of time. Wholly successful, it was achieved without a script.

When the composer has been put to work— *composers* is more accurate, for, as a general rule, she has during this period two plays on her mind, unrelated in characters, action, and theme—Martha touches ground again for a while. She begins to worry about the repertory and casting problems and either at the School or at her apartment she spends hours on the telephone talking to the members of the company, finding out who is available, who is not, trying to woo a recalcitrant back, assessing the difficulties the answers pose.

Although many months or a year or more may have passed since they have worked together, she usually finds that the dancers are available, or are willing to make themselves so. Since its beginning in 1927, the company as an entity, performing a changing and growing repertory, has remained remarkably intact. Many dancers later to be choreographers, among them Sophie Maslow, May O'Donnell, Erick Hawkins, Pearl Lang, Merce Cunningham, John Butler, and Paul Taylor, grew to maturity in the company and left, asserting not necessarily their independence of Martha and her art, but their independence with it and the freedom she herself had claimed to go their own ways. Some, equally mature, have found it possible for

OPPOSITE: *Appalachian Spring:* Matt Turney, Robert Cohan, Ethel Winter, and Company.

BELOW: *Cave of the Heart:* Helen McGehee

the past twenty years and more to keep their independence and to be artists on their own terms while they continued to work with her and to make an inestimable contribution to her theater. They are the stars of her company.

Helen McGehee, Ethel Winter, and Yuriko have been with the company since the mid-forties. Helen, a Virginian, graduated Phi Beta Kappa in Greek from Randolph-Macon; Ethel comes from Boston and graduated from Bennington; Yuriko, a Nisei, born in California, educated in Japan, confined in a West Coast detention camp for a time during World War II, was working as a seamstress on Seventh Avenue when she first came to study with Martha. Except that they are, as are the other major members of the company, each in her own way masters of the technique, expert teachers and choreographers, they are as little alike as these plain facts of their backgrounds imply.

Helen is intellectual. She has a strict, logical mind and a critical eye. Her bent is toward precision and exactitude and this shapes her movements as a dancer; they are finely drawn, like etchings on space. Yet there is a wealth of feeling in her, currents of violence and tenacious loyalties that come fully to light when she plays Electra in *Clytemnestra.*

Though she has a good tough streak and a sly sense of humor and of the absurd, Ethel is deeply feminine. For a long time, her great patrician beauty and her way of moving had an aura of poignance; she was like a princess under a spell in a legend whose end was by no means certain to be happy, and she still perfectly projects this quality when, playing the part of Helen of Troy,

she paces the battlements, looking down upon the rape of the town. But somewhere along the line the spell was broken and now as she goes from Helen to Saint Joan to the vicious Aphrodite in *Phaedra,* there seems to be no limit to her range.

In both beauty and temperament, Yuriko is a rich mixture of East and West. On stage, she is like an exotic flower, an intricate tropical blossom whose tough roots go deep; offstage, she is volatile but commonsensical, a woman of granitic convictions which she expresses in a startling strident Bronx accent. When she tackles a role, whether Iphigenia or the wayward Eve in *Embattled Garden* or the Maid in *Seraphic Dialogue,* she goes about it with the singlemindedness and ferocity of Bushido and years may pass before she decides that she is finally doing a good job.

Mary Hinkson and Matt Turney joined the company in 1951. Mary is from Philadelphia, Matt is from Americus, Georgia; both are Negroes, both the daughters of doctors, both graduates of the University of Wisconsin; there the similarities end. Mary is hard-headed and down to earth; Matt is evanescent, a guest in the here and now. Mary, Martha says, has "the perfect dancer's body . . . perfect feet." Matt is Modigliani's ideal; if he had ever seen her, he might never have painted any other model or, perhaps, seeing his vision perfectly realized in the flesh, he might never have painted again. Mary's gift is for an exquisite lyricism which seems to spring out of an enormous bridled power; Matt's is unique and indescribable.

In 1965, Martha chose Helen to play Medea in the restoration of *Cave of the Heart;* Yuriko to play the Virgin in Primitive Mysteries; and Ethel to play the bride in *Appalachian Spring.* She created *Part Real—Part Dream* for Mary and Matt; to see them together on stage in that fairy tale is almost a surfeit of loveliness.

Linda Hodes was born of Jewish parents in New York City and she was a child when she came to study at the Graham School. She is darkly beautiful; a lithe, predominantly sensuous being and

closer in this than any of the others to that side of Martha's nature. Her performance of the role of Saint Joan is radically different from Ethel's; her Cassandra is radically different from Matt's, yet both are equally valid and moving. As the young Judith, the chaste seductress, she is at her best.

Of these six stars, five have been married successfully for a number of years; divorce is very rare among Graham dancers. Four are mothers, very good ones, whose children seem not to have been in the least distracted by their mothers' careers. Otherwise, patently, they have nothing in common but the things Martha delights in: their artistry, strength of character, and intense individuality. This is equally true of the company's male stars.

There are five of them: Robert Powell, the youngest, is from Hawaii; Gene McDonald is from Nebraska; David Wood from the state of Washington; and Robert Cohan and Bertram Ross are both New Yorkers.

Bob Powell is slight of build and quiet and, off stage, seems frail; on stage, he is or soon may be a *danseur noble.* Martha has spoken about moments in her theater which she "treasures," split-seconds of action she finds herself on the alert for; one of these is Bob's leap early in *Acrobats of God.*

Gene McDonald is elusive. Tall, gaunt, he has the look and something of the mood and strength of a Giacommetti sculpture, qualities Martha made full use of when she created for him the quadruple role of King Hades-The Watchman-Paris-The Ghost of Agamemnon in *Clytemnestra.*

David Wood is stocky, hard-driving, a stern disciplinarian. His role in *Acrobats of God,* the whip-cracking ringmaster, is not difficult for him to play: he has been the company's régisseur for several years.

Robert Cohan came to study at the School soon after the war ended. He had been critically wounded in the Battle of the Bulge and he took up dance as physical therapy but after a few months he was performing with the company and he has stayed with it off and on ever since. He is tall (Martha prefers to work with men who are six feet tall or more), handsome in a romantic, turn-of-the-century way, and he has the temperament and style to match. He shares Martha's bent toward mysticism; he is interested in Gurdjieff, extrasensory perception, and Huxley's experiments with mescaline. He is very serious about acting and, like Yuriko, he is usually in a state of dissatisfaction about the details of his performances. He is an ideal Theseus, noble and distraught, in *Phaedra;* a fine, slinky Stranger in *Embattled Garden;* and a fine, decadent Aegisthus in *Clytemnestra;* but he may be too handsome, too clearly the perfect romantic hero, to be entirely convincing when plain, straightforward evil is called for.

Bertram Ross is convincing when anything is called for. Like Bob Cohan, he came to the School as a veteran of World War II. He was already an accomplished pianist and an accomplished painter. He joined the company in 1947 and since then there has not been a performance anywhere in the world in which he did not appear. He has risen gradually to dominate absolutely, with Martha, every performance and at this point the curtain could not go up if Bert were not present and ready. In 1963 there was only one work in the repertory, *Secular Games,* he did not appear in; in all the others he played central roles. He is a wonderfully complex man, deeply serious, hilariously comical. When the going gets rough, his clowning gets everybody through. Of all the company, he is the least demanding, the easiest to work with. Although he is a marathon talker, he is, of all of them, within himself the quietest. He is certainly the most versatile actor-dancer alive, and there is no indication that Martha could ever, as a dramatist, exhaust his gifts. Her present theater is built around him. He plays both the pompous, arrogant Agamemnon and the tragic Orestes in *Clytemnestra.* He is the compassionate St. Michael in *Seraphic Dialogue,* Oedipus in *Night Journey,* Adam in *Embattled Garden,* Holofernes in *Legend of Judith.* He is the poetic dancer Martha flirts with, protects, and rejects in *Acrobats of God;* the betrayed Hippolytus in *Phaedra;* and the young lover in *Diversion of Angels.* During its Broadway seasons, the company usually does seven performances between Friday and Sunday; this usually means that Bert will appear in fifteen different roles. No other living performer is required to do so much; Bert likes it.

Bert and Bob played the male leads in the two new plays Martha did in 1965. In *Part Real—Part Dream* she cast Bob as a considerably more complex "Stranger" and Bert as a deeper Adam and their confrontation takes place in another kind of Eden, a "holy jungle" that looks strikingly like a Persian garden of pleasure. In *The Witch of Endor* Bob is the young King David, the chosen usurper, and Bert is King Saul: taking a significant step away from the expected, Martha built the play so that, in spite of her presence as the Witch, they dominate it.

As a group, the younger members of the company are as motley as the stars: Takako Asakawa is from Tokyo, Juliet Fisher from New Zealand, Noemi Lapzeson from Argentina; Carol Fried and Phyllis Gutelius are New Yorkers; Clive Thompson is Jamaican, Peter Randazzo, Sicilian-American,

ABOVE: *Secular Games:* Robert Powell and Company
RIGHT: *Cave of the Heart:* Yuriko, Robert Cohan,
Helen McGehee, and Matt Turney

from Brooklyn; Dudley Williams, Gus Solomon, Jr., and William Louther, Negroes, are from New York.

The company is generally intelligent (Martha demands it), well-informed, well-read; they have cultivated tastes but, as individuals, few common interests and away from the School and work, they rarely get together. There are few close friendships among them. Most do have in common a lack of money; they lead frugal lives. As teachers they are, perforce, underpaid. As performers they usually earn less than the musician in the pit and the electrician backstage. If it were not for unemployment insurance, many of them would have to give up dancing. Nevertheless, they are usually good-humored, high-spirited, quick to laugh, and when they come together to work they give themselves wholly to it. To an outsider, they might seem the most dedicated, unselfish, and patient of human beings, but they do not see themselves this way. They are clear-headed about what they are doing and why they are doing it and they know the cost in time, energy, money, fury, and tears.

Their commitment to Martha's art keeps them together, but they were chosen in the first place because of their differences, their unique qualities as individuals which caught Martha's eye and which promised her as a dramatist rich potentialities. At this point, she knows them so thoroughly and so intimately that they must work in her imagination in the earliest phase of the creative process inseparably from the characters of the developing play. They must be dancing long before they know it. This causes problems, artistic and personal. The stars of the company hope, naturally enough, for important roles in the new

works; the younger members hope to be elevated. Martha does not like to disappoint them. She frets. She goes over meticulously the casting of the repertory and judges whether the stars will be seen to advantage often enough during the limited performance period; if it seems that one or the other will not be, then she begins to change her thinking. Though up to now this dancer or that may not have figured at all in the growth of the new plays, she will decide to add roles, so that no one feels slighted. This suggests a willingness on her part to compromise the idea and, perhaps, the finished work of art and it is true that some of her plays have been marred by the presence of extraneous characters; trying to please everybody, she ended in not pleasing anybody, not even the dancers concerned, for they are the first to know when she arbitrarily creates a role because she thinks they need or deserve one. But what underlies this willingness to compromise the work of art is her unwillingness to jeopardize the working relationships which make her theater possible. If, for the stars of the company, a balance were not kept in their appearances and positions on the stage, they would go one by one. Martha is the only person who can keep this balance and most often she succeeds, to the degree that the problem of billing, knotty in any theatrical enterprise, becomes for her company, except for Bertram Ross, whose position as male star no one questions, next to insoluble. When she fails, it is practically speaking worth it; she and the company do go on working together, as they have done for a longer time than any other repertory group. But then there is in this, as in all other situations where Martha is concerned, another side fraught with woe: she may, out of the blue and for no reason anyone ever knows, lose interest in a dancer or turn against one or another of them, implacably and surely irrationally against, and then the foundations of her theater do quake. Dispensing favors and benevolence, she is imperious and often incomprehensible; she is equally imperious in withholding them and in temporary excommunication.

With the play and the dancers in her head, but lacking the new music that will weld them, Martha begins to prowl around the School, as though in its spaces and the past uses she had put them to she finds present reassurance. There is an ample but low-ceilinged studio on the third floor where in the late mornings she may sometimes be found working alone on the technique. Until very recently, she insisted that she was in no condition to perform unless she could do 400 jumps in 15 minutes without being winded. The second floor is given over to a dressing room for women students and to the School office. The latter is cramped, sorely inconvenient, and lighted by naked glaring bulbs; Martha avoids it. On the ground floor at the front of the building there is a studio of generous size which, during the rehearsal and performance period, is likely to be used for everything but dance classes. It is a storage room for sets, props, and crates; a handyman's workshop; a wardrobe room where the costumes are designed and where seamstresses work, often around the clock. In the left-over space, on random uncomfortable chairs and low benches, the dancers try to rest between rehearsals and fittings. Adjoining this studio, there is a small room, a

bath, a double-decker storage closet for costumes and a cramped L-shaped kitchen. These walled spaces make a warren. Once, the small room with bath was supposed to be Martha's; the bath still is hers in a way and she may retreat there on occasion; there is no privacy anywhere else. The room is now choked with the overflow from her library, with discarded furniture, unusable desks and broken lamps; it is supposed to be an "office." The kitchen is a gathering place for the teachers and the dancers and it is usually impassable. In the gathering jumble, she finds much to curse about, much that is creatively vexing.

The "big studio," at the rear of the building, is reserved, except for classes, for her use. There, when the first sections of music come from the composer—weeks, sometimes months before regular rehearsals of the repertory are underway— she begins to work with Eugene Lester, her musical director. Martha cannot read music; she claims she cannot tell one printed note from the other. She is not, in the accepted sense, a lover of music. She never goes, except under duress, to concerts or to the opera. She does not own a phonograph. In short, she never listens to music for the pleasure of it. Her approach to it is strictly professional and masterly and simple. She listens to her new scores over and over and over again until the patterns, rhythms, pulsations are, as she says, in her "sinews"; literally, physically so. Her sinews, rather than her brain and the apparatus of memory, absorb the music and are permeated by it and this seems to happen very quickly. Working from the piano reduction, she hears soon how the score will sound when the orchestra plays it and precisely calculates at each moment its dramatic effect. She is quickly able to say to Eugene, "Go back to the flute solo," the trumpets, the cello. She allows herself to be guided by the composer; it is likely that she even enjoys now the domination and the restrictions his music impose upon her. She never tampers with it, never violates his tempi, rarely if ever asks him to make changes or to adjust to what she might earlier have imagined as suitable to her own designs. She may become restive against a certain passage, may be irritated by a thematic development, but eventually she will manage to turn her restiveness and irritation to advantage. Composers have sat in the theater and watched amazed at the way she has used their musical ideas. Many insist that she invariably illuminates their work for them, finding in it what they themselves did not know was there. She achieves this by an indefinable, certainly non-rational method; the music, usually difficult and of the highest sophistication, takes her body over, she submits, but only in order finally to dominate.

There is a sure sign when she has "the pattern of the composition" in her sinews. Wide double doors open into the big studio: she ties their handles together with a strip of cloth, usually red jersey, and everyone on the premises knows what that means. From now on, no one unasked enters until the knot is untied. It does not deter the students from peeking through the crack. Often there are five or six of them there, clustered in positions from a squat to tip-toe, but they do not see much for the studio gets little daylight and Martha seems to prefer to work during this phase in a thick gloom. What they may see is a dancer or two moving around in the center space and, far across, Martha, seated on a low bench against the wall between two long reaches of mirror, huddled in a shawl to keep off the cold she says she always feels when she is doing a new work.

There in the gloom she has begun, in the words of one of her most fervent supporters and admirers, the person who understands her best, to fulfill "her basic need: act as a medium, live her own law, and conquer the world." Martha would acknowledge the truth and precision of this formulation, even the part about conquering the world. As an artist, she has always felt herself to be a medium through which the creative force works and she is and always has been a most willing instrument; between the laws of the creative force and her own laws, there have been only minor skirmishes. In her words, she has begun now to "build a vision" and the act of building is "like fitting together the infinitesmal pieces of a mosaic." Visions are insubstantial, fleeting; mosaics are stone and endure. Despite the contradiction, this is, poetically speaking—as she most often does—very close to the truth of what is happening. Her finished plays are a succession of visions which add up to a single whole vision and each, fixed in the instant, is fitted to the next and related with it as are the fragments of a mosaic. Each, lifted out—as she has done on occasion, allowing to be performed or performing herself a solo or duet or group dance—is unavoidably a fragment; there is unfilled space around it. Removed from the play, it is reduced, so to speak, to a speech or a brief scene played without benefit of what came before, what specific action

brought about this unique ecstasy or this unique rage. It is effective, but it is only part of a whole and one feels the lack.

Acting as a medium, living her own law, on her bench in the murky light, Martha is situated dead center of the microcosm of which she is the efficient and material cause and, having begun to build a new vision, she has started in that microcosm another evolution. As an act of creation, there is little or no serenity about it: much closer to the Hindu than to the Old Testament idea of how worlds come into being and evolutions are achieved, it is all a clanging and clashing of opposites.

Martha is a very small, thin woman, shy of strangers, uncertain of herself in public, uncomfortable in the company of all but those few who are closest to her. To the grocer, the delivery boy, the maid, the saleswoman, the taxi-cab driver, she is soft-spoken and invariably courteous; "a real lady," "a great lady," who is surprised and pleased if they know who she is. To her audiences who crowd backstage after a performance, she is, no matter how great an ovation they have given her, humble, grateful, and warmly welcoming. To her closer acquaintances, those who have admired and supported her for years, she is a puzzle, for she never seeks them out. She seems never to have relied on those who feel they are her friends. If she accepts their invitations, she may very well at the last minute back out; if she goes, it is with reluctance. She feels her way into social occasions as if she had wandered onto a stage into a role she does not know in a play whose plot is a mystery to her, and it is then plain to see how thoroughly

the lone artist and how little the star she is and how exceedingly difficult it must be for her to confront the opacity of fame. But it is impossible for anyone to be prepared for her: she may arrive and play the star, the queen, the conqueror to the hilt.

The few who are closest to her are those people with whom she works day in and day out and with them she is warm, simple, inexhaustibly interested in the minutiae of their lives, quick to smile and to laugh, generous, even Lady Bountiful, the quickest to respond to trouble or need; the best, most calm, and clearest headed in times of real crisis. Or, especially when she is situated at the center of things, she is totally unpredictable. Sometimes, compared with her, mercury is a staid and stolid substance. One learns quickly—and this may be true for any artist in varying degrees according to his range, temperament, and "basic need"—that for Martha a peaceful atmosphere and a smooth path ahead, whether interior or exterior, are inimical to the creative process. Friction, tension, head-on battles are indispensable. In racing terms, Martha cannot possibly run on a dry track and she is not even comfortable on a muddy one; she runs best in a bog.

Added to the opposites of her heritage, immediate background, and upbringing which have led her to her themes, there are those most artists know and suffer: energy versus primordial inertia; flights of fancy versus the disciplined imagination; the sense of being the prey of the bird in flight versus the sense of absolute power if only the means can be found to wield it; independence, without which nothing may be accomplished, but paid for in loneliness of an intensity unimaginable

to most of humankind. This last, this independence and indispensable isolation of the artist as he works, is the source of a conflict in Martha which most artists do not experience and out of it comes the most furious clashing.

Any theatrical venture is, of course, cooperative. Martha's work begins to be cooperative the moment she hands her script to the composer and it becomes increasingly so until, by curtain time on opening night, a hundred or so people are involved. It must have been from the beginning extremely difficult for her to cope with this fact:

as a dramatist, one who would by nature fight the world for privacy and isolation in order to be able to work, she, by contrast, must work increasingly in public and the closer she comes to the most difficult part of her creative task, the realization of the idea, the development of the drama through movement alone, the more she comes under the scrutiny of a crowd of eyes. All choreographers come under this scrutiny as they work out their ideas with their dancers, but none on the scene at present is a dramatist and that makes all the difference. Martha has often insisted that she is not a choreographer at all; she has said recently that she is not even sure she is a dancer. Coming from her, this would be brazen if she did not seriously mean it and if it didn't, in a certain way, make sense. With few exceptions, the choreographer designs patterns of movement, inside or outside of a formal tradition, which are meant to be exciting and aesthetically satisfying but which bear little or no weight of meaning. For Martha, it is the reverse: dancing, she is an actress; "choreographing," she is a dramatist, vulnerable, fully exposed when the work is hardest.

At the same time, it is in the nature of things that she is being forced to relinquish her independence. The farther she goes on her own and the closer she comes to that point at which the creative force fully takes her over and she becomes "a medium," "an instrument," the more dependent she becomes on the company and the more dependent she becomes the more she fights.

Ultimately, Martha makes it as clear as anyone could do that the creative process is itself as much a matter of destruction as of creation; that, as an artist in the midst of that process, something is being destroyed inside of her, some feature of her inner landscape, so that something else may come into being, and if the destruction is to be bearable it must somehow be projected into the world around her. In the process, everyday notions of right and wrong, proper and improper, good and bad, cruel and kind go out the window. The climate of her relationships may change in an instant: a single blast of wind may freeze solid what had been mild green country; sunlight may fall suddenly into a place long dark and chilly. It is now that some dancer will get her fixed attention while another becomes the target of steady attack. Mercurial, irresponsible in ordinary human terms, only explicable in that it all reflects what is going on inside of her and the extent to which she has given way to the demands of her own creativity. The dancers and the others who work with her understand and survive admirably, some with permanent wounds, but none of them is naïve enough to think that the world, especially theirs, is an easy place, and some know that their scars are valuable. In fact, everyone around Martha worries if the weather is too pleasant: the more she gives way, the more she plays the range of her limitless temperament, rages and subsides, fights her dependencies and shifts them, the more likely it seems to be that the new play will be among her best.

Martha is not of course solely responsible for the bog. The dancers are richly temperamental themselves and their basic differences as people make for considerable friction. There are jealousies, rivalries, and old grudges which put considerable additional strain on the nerves. But then tensions ease and the storms abate and the weather turns pleasant. Times of gaiety help to offset the woe.

Working, Martha often sinks into long spells of silence. She usually wears for work an ankle-length black practise dress and black tights. Her favorite shawl is a beige, very soft Pushmini she bought in India; she pulls it around her, tucks her feet under and all but vanishes. At such times, she looks so small and frail that it is hard not to rush in or fly up and try to save her before she is taken forever away. In the silence, the dancers wait, slumped against the piano, propped against the walls, sprawled on the floor, singly, in clumps, in heaps, and they look like a bankrupt circus act. Some seem to share Martha's cold and wear a variety of sweaters, sweat-shirts, knitted wool leg-warmers the Goodwill Industries would turn down. The finest legs are encumbered by kneepads; feet bear big patches of adhesive. They wear tights and leotards of various colors and these are usually old, snagged, with holes and runners. In such garments, which would seem to defy Martha to conjure up anything beautiful, they loll in postures so graceless that, if it were not common knowledge that dancers are rarely graceful except when dancing, no one could believe them capable of performing an acceptable fox-trot. Early in their tour of the Orient, they won an admirer named Felix, the pilot of the plane which flew them from Tokyo to Manila to Bangkok. Felix never watched the performances from the house; he stood each night unobtrusively in the wings, rivetted. He said he preferred the place backstage because he could only see there a discovery he had made: the dancers were like his plane. On the ground it lumbered, it was heavy, hard to handle, but the instant it gained the air it seemed weightless . . . just so the dancers lumbered, waddled, toward the stage and then, on cue, out and up into the light they went.

Instead of lolling in the silence, some of them may quietly try to work out whatever the problem is on their own. They know now something about the shape of the vision or, if not its shape, at least its atmosphere. Martha lends them books she has been reading, shows them poems or pictures she has come across which have moved her toward the feeling and scene she wants, talks to them in her evocative way about the characters they will enact; gives them, in short, an ambience of poetic substance to move in. Thus, she works with the company as earlier she worked with the composer and vastly widens the space the play grows in by allowing the dancers freedom for their own inventiveness and creativity. Often, while they experiment, she leaves the studio; often they set up rehearsal times to work without her, devising patterns of movement she will judge later. She testifies to this in *Acrobats of God,* in those sequences in which the dancers, still on one level figments of her imagination and of what she as artist can think up to do, are yet on another level on their own, showing her what they can do while, from behind her mirror or perched on the barre, she very carefully takes note. She has asked on a number of occasions that this collaboration with the dancers and the contribution they make to her works be publicly acknowledged; that the credits read "Choreography by Martha Graham and the Company." They have declined, not out of any misguided humility, but out of their conviction that the whole vision, the play as finally performed, is the significant thing and that the play is Martha's.

Sometimes, Martha leaves the quiet studio by a small side door and goes searching through the building for some object: a pole, a length of rope, a prop from an earlier work, a length of cloth, an old costume, a chair or stool of a certain height, anything that may suggest for the moment what she needs. To a degree, this is the making-do everyone puts up with in the theater until the finished props and set are available. Throughout the choreographing period, a tall aluminum ladder was made to serve as the cloud Circe rests upon. But for Martha it is significantly more than making-do: the objects she scavenges quickly become a vital part of the play.

In our theater, realistic or poetic, even the most experimental, the scene of the action is the material world and the characters act out the drama within a setting that is a facsimile of that world, an inert background with which they have as little essential relation as anyone has with his daily surroundings. The objects they handle are what they are: a cup is a cup, a glass a glass, a sword a sword, etc. When the playwright invests an object with symbolic meaning, he usually does it on the basis of what the object is. Beckett's ash cans, for example, are as realistic and ultimately as inert a setting as any designed for a drawing-room comedy. On the classical stage, whether the Globe or the Noh or the amphitheatre at Delphi, a single unit suffices, of course, for all varieties of action; the material world is handled by the poetry and, consequently, is vastly more meaningful and active in the drama. Through a consensus about the nature of man and the universe, the dramatic poet could put objects to work: in the *Oresteia,* the cloak Clytemnestra offers Agamemnon as a gift upon his return in triumph from Troy is not only magnificent, it is purple, the color of the gods, and when, in pride and arrogance, he allows himself to be wheedled into stepping down upon that color he is on the instant doomed. This is Martha's mode of thinking. Invincibly humanistic, holding unshakeable convic-

tions about the existence of God and the validity of spiritual experience, she was forced to set to work as a dramatist in a world which lacks any such consensus, in which symbolic thinking is highly suspect, in which language itself—or the poetic mind in using it—had lost much of its power over materiality. With the inner, immaterial life of the human being as her obsessive concern, she solved her problem by simply banishing the material, recognizable world from her stage. The action of her plays always takes place in the mind, heart, and soul of her characters; her unshakeable premise is that, if the Kingdom of God is within, so then is reality. There is nothing new in this either for the artist or the philosopher, but Martha alone has found the way fully to convey it and probe its limits in drama. A number of factors are involved in this achievement, the abandonment of language being one of them, but the signal one is her approach to the stage. In banishing the material world, she abandoned stage settings and properties as such, rejected scenic backdrops and painted flats and gave herself thereby an immensity of space into which she placed objects and sculptured shapes, usually abstract, which are invested with meaning by the action itself. She stripped the stage of literal, recognizable things or, if she used such a thing, she quickly stripped it of its literalness. The coiled rope Jocasta holds high when the curtain rises on *Night Journey* is the rope she will hang herself with, but it is used at once to introduce a character and a theme: Tiresias comes, stabbing the earth with his blindman's staff, and he plunges the staff through the coils, tears the rope from her grip and thus causes the action by forcing her to live the tragedy. The rope vanishes but reappears near the climax of the play to become the umbilical cord which once tied Oedipus to Jocasta and now ties them again. Finally it becomes the image of the web of their fate. Tiresias, bringing the truth, cuts his way through that web and turns the action back to its beginning, in the instant before Jocasta's death, but now, when she picks up the rope, it has become a poetic symbol dense with the whole meaning of the play. Tiresias's staff is not, either, simply a staff: resounding as it stabs the earth, it is the truth pounding into Jocasta's mind and at the end, it sounds the last beats of her heart.

Underlying the complexity and richness of these simple objects, there is the directness and freedom of a child's imagination; it is part of Martha's genius that she is still, somewhere in her inner world, a little girl play-acting, making things be what she wishes them to be. In *Clytemnestra,* the cape she offers Agamemnon is some twenty feet long and five feet wide; it is a little girl's dream of the grandest cape a queen could wear and Martha wears it that way, but later she turns it into the curtains over the doorway of the palace at Mycenae and allows them to be parted to reveal Clytemnestra's acts of murder and then she turns it into funeral drapery on the cart which bears the victims away. In the first of the dialogues in *Seraphic Dialogue,* Joan the Maid wears a peasant girl's dress for a solo which is a distillation as economical and evocative in its movement design as the finest poetry, of the story of the girlhood of Joan of Arc, and, by extension, the essence of all girlhood on the brink of womanhood and of destiny, no matter whether high or low. The phases of the story are conveyed by the use of a kerchief, blue on one side, white on the other. As the Maid, having heard her saints' voices for the first time, sets timidly out within herself to do their bidding, she covers her head with the kerchief, showing blue, and walks, a simple girl with visions, the long way away from Lorraine. When, awestruck, she hears the voices again and knows that she is about to be torn away from all she has known of herself and the world, the kerchief, now white, becomes her maidenhead, her innocence and frailty; as she dreams of the glory of battle, it becomes her banner, whipping blue and white in the wind. At the height of that dream, her voices speak again, the kerchief falls from her fingers and youth and innocence fall with it, she falls and lies stricken as if she has been ravaged, and when she rises and tucks the kerchief at her waist she is a maid no longer. Her destiny is upon her.

For Agamemnon in *Clytemnestra,* Martha thought up towering, gold-bladed spears. A pair of them, crossed, first appears in the Prologue (it is an Act if ever there was one, but Martha prefers to call it a Prologue) and as Clytemnestra sees them they are the rack upon which Iphigenia was sacrificed. Two pairs of them, crossed, appear in Act I, in the first phase of Clytemnestra's long meditation upon the news of Agamemnon's return to Mycenae; now carried lengthwise, they are the gates of her memory and as they cross and recross the stage, in the shifting, floating way of memory, she sees herself and Aegisthus between them, walking toward each other, meeting in their first encounter, passing as though in the limitless corridor of time. She sees Helen and Paris meet between them and pass, then Iphigenia and her executioner. As her vision comes into finer focus, the pairs of spears are set in place to frame, in bitter and ironical juxtaposition, Aegisthus and herself, in their abandon, the courtship of Helen and Paris, and the ritual sacrifice of Iphigenia. When next seen, a pair of the spears serves as Agamemnon's triumphal chariot and then as the cart upon which his body and Cassandra's are taken away. In Act II, it serves as the rack upon which the tortured ghost of Agamemnon writhes in Clytemnestra's nightmare and finally, locked to the throne, it towers over the action, symbolic of the imminent fact that the throne is no longer hers and that she will die.

This playfulness in dead earnest shapes one of the central characters in *Clytemnestra.* In Act I, King Hades, stripped of the mask he wears throughout the Prologue, becomes the Watchman who sights the beacon fires and announces the fall of Troy and so the fall of the house of Mycenae. Then he becomes Paris and in Act II he is ghost of Agamemnon and in the Epilogue he is again King Hades.

Much of the meaning of *Alcestis* is to be found in the massive set pieces on the stage and the way they are handled. A huge stone wheel and a structure which suggests the stone masonry of the Lion Gate of Mycenae, they were originally designed by Noguchi for the film of *Night Journey.* When the film was completed, they were brought to the School and stored in the big studio. Their looming bulk, the fact that they were obstacles she was forced daily to shove around and that, despite

their look, they were very light in weight, must have begun to work on her imagination early and to affect her thinking about *Alcestis* for, by the time she was ready to do the play, she brought them directly into the action and made it revolve around them. When the curtain rises, the scene is a place of stone, huge, immovable, crushing the spirit. Eerily, the gate-like structure begins to turn, Thanatos reveals himself, and the effect is one of even greater weight and oppression. But then, when he has taken Alcestis down toward death, some kind of death not necessarily physical, a flower is thrust through the axle-hole of the stone wheel and Hercules appears to show that the wheel is weightless, a plaything for him, and the rest of the play is concerned with easing the weight of things and dispelling the mortal oppression. This is accomplished as Hercules and the other characters toy with the stony objects, sliding them around the stage, turning them upside down, setting them on their side—at one point, the wheel becomes the banquet table where Hercules and Admetus revel; and at another, set upright, it is the refuge where Alcestis hides when Hercules fights Thanatos—in a kind of celebration which changes whatever winter of the soul into the warmth and lightness of spring.

Diversion of Angels is played on a bare stage against a sky-blue backdrop. In *Secular Games* there are some low free-form mounds which suggest tiny islands or steppingstones and the only recognizable object is a fanciful ball the men play with. The setting for *Seraphic Dialogue,* surely one of the most beautiful ever to be seen in the theater, is an abstraction in brass tubing which suggests a resplendent, light-filled Gothic cathedral. The complexities of *Clytemnestra* are worked out on a stage very nearly bare, though in memory it seems an opulent production. In *Night Journey,* there is a white free-form stool and a set of graduated blocks of various shapes leading up to a "bed" which is more like a rack, steeply slanted; closely examined, it proves to be an abstraction of male and female conjoined.

Watching Martha's plays, one has inescapably the sense of observing *natural* events, courses of action that are a part of and are taking place directly within a natural order. Put at its simplest, one's sense of wonder is a child's as he looks into an aquarium: strange though the inhabitants and their framed world may be, everything there is rightfully there, everything works with everything else, nothing may be dispensed with. To achieve this *naturalness,* one of Martha's strategies is to use an abstract object as a place for a character, a home base where the character is first discovered and to which, throughout the action, he returns, so that at last the poetic import of the character and of the object, the specific *experience* of both, are, in the imagination of the spectator, all but inseparable. In *Legend of Judith,* what serves as the aged, questioning Judith's place is a simulated stone structure that is like an arid promontory, a cliff edge which overhangs a curved ledge. Upon and around this structure, much of the past-but-present action occurs, including the seduction and murder of Holofernes, and its stark aspect as the place where the heroine now is underscores and even vitalizes the theme. In *Phaedra,* Hippolytus's place is a tall, flat, standing object of black metal with blue apertures which, when opened, first reveal him. In Phaedra's mind, it is a living icon of the object of her lust and of its consequences: when Hippolytus is dead, he is placed inside it and the apertures are closed upon his image. Downstage left is another standing object: another icon, it is Aphrodite's place, and it suggests both the avid womb and the shell she emerged from out of the sea. The tragedy's currents surge relentlessly between these two icons until, at the climax, they are made fully visible, as though black dye had been poured into a clear rushing stream: in a vision, Phaedra sees Pasiphaë, her mother, caught high in a swirl of black net which symbolizes both the bull that covered her and the extremity of lust. At the end of the tragedy, Phaedra lies dead in that swirl of black and Aphrodite's icon is left open to reveal the goddess with her legs spread wide.

NIGHT JOURNEY

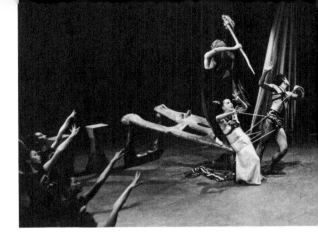

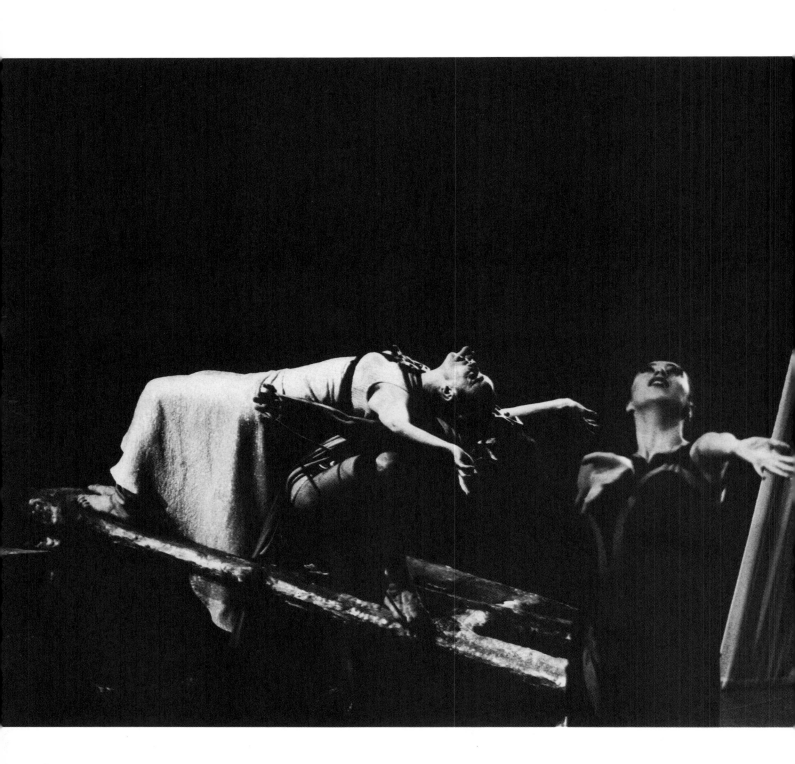

CLYTEMNESTRA

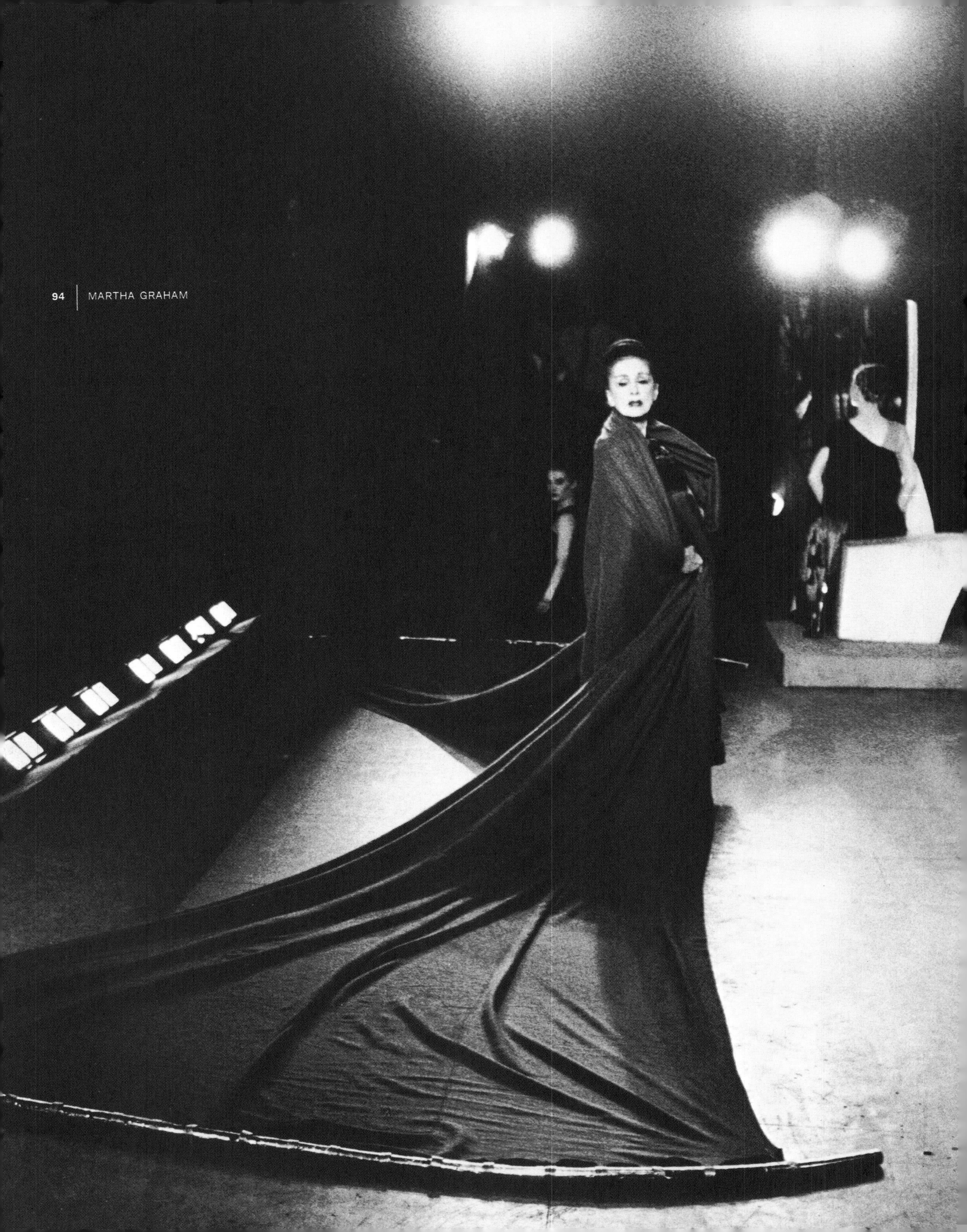

ALCESTIS

PHAEDRA

During the first three weeks of November, 1965, with the restoration to her repertory of *Primitive Mysteries,* which dates from 1931, *Appalachian Spring,* from 1944, and *Cave of the Heart,* from 1946, Martha's audiences had an opportunity for the first time, and very likely the last, to observe in retrospect among many other things her development as a master of stage space and of the use of stage decor for dramatic purposes. The other things are what make it likely that the opportunity will not be offered again. Martha detests the thought of reviving her works. The quintessential artist, she is neither sentimental nor nostalgic about her past achievements; as a woman, she is, however, protective of them against others. She views them as though they were seashells she grew to live in for a time, then shed on a stretch of beach she has no intention of ever going back to. Nor shall anyone else. Besides, she is always changing, always growing new shells and to that process the past is clearly a threat. The thought is made more detestable to her by the fact that her greatest works, those the world is demanding now to see again, were her most deeply personal statements, signal adventures in the course of her private myth. Naturally enough, she does not want to relive them and the world is scarcely justified in expecting her, as artist, to do it, or in expecting her, as woman gracefully and generously to relinquish to others, younger, those hard-won secrets which transformed her, let alone the hard-won glory which comes with having created and, in her case, being the vital center of a masterpiece. Then there is the labor that is required, the plain drudgery. She has created 139 works for the stage.

None has been notated, and it is difficult to see how notation could be of much value, for, though it could record the sequences of movement, it could scarcely indicate what Martha refers to as the "distortion of the absolute of the technique," the subtle stylization which is developed in each play and is peculiar to it alone, nor could it in any reliable way indicate, since her works are plays, the dramatic demands she made upon her dancers. Only two of her works, *Night Journey* and *Appalachian Spring,* have been filmed for the general public and this happened only because Nathan Kroll, the film producer who had earlier made Martha's great film *A Dancer's World* possible, was determined on it. As for the rest, the records are patchy or simply non-existent. *Frontier* was filmed in 1936 but Martha would not allow it to be released. There is a short film in circulation which purports to be *Lamentation,* one of her early great solos, but it is in fact a pastiche of poses she did for a sculptor, not the dance at all. In recent years, including 1965, the repertory then current was recorded on film under crude conditions for use in rehearsal; many of the older prints are now worn to shreds and no one seems to know where the negatives might be located. This means that by far the greater portion of Martha's contribution to the theater has vanished and present and future generations may know of it only as legend. Aside from the notes the accompanist makes on his score when the fragments of the "mosaic" are "set," there is usually no record of the play except in Martha's and the dancer's memories. There were not even accompanist's notes for *Primitive Mysteries* and it had not been performed for fif-teen years; it was restored, under Sophie Maslow's direction, from memory by Martha and others of the corps of dancers who had first performed it. The effort to remember the moment by moment, gesture by gesture, progress of works of such complexity (Martha calls *Primitive Mysteries* a "cruel" dance, and it is) is agonizing and to her scarcely worth it. Finally, there is the audience sitting there, some of them vividly remembering. Martha's fame rests not only upon her dramatic creations but upon her interpretations of them; upon the intense mesmerizing power of what, as she performed, seemed not to be an interpretation but itself an act of creation. The secrets of that immediate power were hidden in the plays themselves, in the very fact that they were shells she chose to grow and inhabit in that time; in her attitude to them, the way she accomodated herself to their convolutions; and in her imponderable self. For herself, she knows that these secrets, these states of being are not recoverable; that, whether or not it is physically possible for her now, she could not play Emily Dickinson or Emily Brontë or the bride in *Appalachian Spring* with the same intense conviction that she brings to Clytemnestra or Judith or the vaporous artist in *Acrobats of God.* Time and the inevitability of her own development have put out those earlier fires. As for the others, the likely inheritors, whatever she might bring herself to tell them now about her heroines and the way she played them would perforce be intellectualization; she would be using words where words were never necessary before, were, in fact, banished by the fundamental precepts of her art. Realistic to her marrow, she knows that all of this

Appalachian Spring: Matt Turney

added up makes revivals of her works a patent impossibility. But restorations are possible, with that word's specific connotation of the new applied to old and venerable things. Anathema though the thought of them is to her, Martha knows as well that, if she does not undertake them or agree to let others attempt it, her life's work in the theater will, except for traces here and there, vanish. Martha the woman might not much care if this happened; Martha the artist must care passionately and she has over the past few years, responding to mounting pressure from the people around her, suffered a few restorations to be done.

Primitive Mysteries, Appalachian Spring, and *Cave of the Heart* caused considerable controversy when they were performed in 1965. Many in the audience who remembered Martha's performances in these works missed her bitterly and thought that without her presence the works had lost stature and should not have been brought back at all. However, the majority, never having seen her in the roles, seemed to find the works and the performances of the younger stars more than acceptable, and for those stars, Yuriko, Ethel Winter, and Helen McGehee, this was close to a triumph, for Martha gave them no help. Yuriko had had some help the summer before, when *Primitive Mysteries* was first restored for a concert at Connecticut College in commemoration of Louis Horst, who wrote the score; Ethel had the film of *Appalachian Spring* to work with; Helen had nothing of *Cave of the Heart* but some patchy notes on the score, some old photographs, and her own phenomenal memory of what Martha had done. Martha refused to give more than a cursory glance at

their rehearsals; she stormed when she heard the music start. Her mind was on *Part Real—Part Dream* and *The Witch of Endor;* in the latter, the Witch was eluding her. She was rehearsing *Clytemnestra, Legend of Judith, Phaedra,* and *Acrobats of God.* Time was short and she had undertaken an inhuman labor. All this aside, that music she was forced to hear was the past; it dragged her back, but at the same time made her agonizingly aware of the present. Old monarchs do not graciously step down; her loathing was immense. Goaded, she did finally appear at the dress rehearsal of *Appalachian Spring.* She sat alone in the theater and no one dared approach her. It is not certain that she watched. When the rehearsal was over, she sat for a long time utterly still and then got up and left the theater without a word. Later in the season she was able to tell the dancers that they had done well and that she was proud of them, but she has spoken often of the pain she endured in her dressing room when the old music came over the loudspeaker and it seems unlikely that she will ever be able to talk seriously and deeply to Yuriko, Ethel, and Helen about what she did in these three works.

But there they were for a time at least on the stage, in something approaching their original state. Each was crucial in her career; each indispensable to an understanding of her art. *Primitive Mysteries* was her final and definitive exploration of the polar influence that Roman Catholicism and the myth of the Virgin had exerted upon her since early childhood. She had danced the role of the Sacrificial Virgin in *Le Sacre du Printemps* in 1930 and it is safe to guess that there was for her a strong poetic logic in the move from the pagan victim, who danced herself to death in order to bring spring, to Mary, God's chosen and willing instrument. The concept of the virgin, the chaste inviolate woman is also, one suspects, inseparable from her experience of herself as an artist. *Primitive Mysteries,* performed on a bare stage, requiring, in addition to the central figure of the Virgin, fourteen women dancers, is cast in the form of a rite, pagan in its intensity, startling in the complexity of its choreographic patterns, startling in the simplicity and directness with which it conveys the impact upon a woman's mind of the myth of the Virgin birth, the Crucifixion and the Resurrection. Regarding stagecraft, it shows that as early as 1931 Martha was already a master; regarding herself as performer, it shows astonishingly—it was her first unquestioned masterpiece —how sure of herself she was: the central figure does almost nothing throughout the dance but pose.

Appalachian Spring, that delightful resolution into lyricism of her struggles with her New England heritage, is played within a set which suggests the bare beginnings of a homestead being built in the wilderness. *Cave of the Heart—* remarkable on its own as an adaptation of the story of Medea; remarkable too in that, as the first play in Martha's Greek cycle, its economy, compression, and dramatic thrust presage all the others— is played within an abstract setting and it shows that by 1946 her mastery of the use of such a setting for dramatic purposes was complete. There are two important objects on the stage: one, at center stage rear, is referred to by the stagehands

as "the elephant's foot" and it rather looks like that, but it serves as the place of the Chorus, an archetypal figure who is both the Nurse of the original drama and the primary observer and interpreter of the action; the other, Medea's place, downstage right, is a structure made of gleaming brass wire resting upon a snake-like base. Spidery, suggesting a nerve center, this piece dominates the stage as no more than Medea's heraldic sign, the emblem at the entrance to her cave, until at the climax, triumphant in her vengeance, she fits herself into it and wears it proudly and one sees how the human soul looks, spiked, forever unapproachable, when fully committed to evil.

Isamu Noguchi is due much of the credit for the wonders Martha has been able to perform with stage decor. He did his first stage design and the first Martha ever used in 1935 for *Frontier.* Although she has collaborated with a number of artists since, including Alexander Calder, who did a huge mobile for her for *Horizons* in 1936, Philip Stapp, Arch Lauterer, Oliver Smith, Frederick Kiesler, Rouben Ter-Arutunian, Jean Rosenthal, and, most recently, Ming Cho Lee and Dani Karavan, she has always worked best with Noguchi. He designed, among others, *Appalachian Spring, Cave of the Heart, Night Journey, Seraphic Dialogue, Clytemnestra, Acrobats of God, Alcestis,* and *Phaedra.* In each he succeeded in making clearly visible and beautiful the inner landscape where the action occurs. Many of the objects he has made for Martha's stage are pure sculptures, works of art in their own right. She would have nothing less and when she is far enough along with a new play and sure of what she needs, she usually begins searching for him. There is a profound empathy between them, a perfect understanding by each of the other's art, a perfect agreement about the use and power of symbols and about the design and use of stage space.

As she does with the composers and with the dancers, she gives Noguchi maximum freedom for his own creativity and gives herself the same freedom to take full advantage of what he produces. When he is available, they get together at her apartment and she tells him what she is planning and, in modest tentatives, what she needs. A few days after, he appears at the School usually carrying a shoebox which contains an infinitesmal mock-up, in paper or carved balsa, of the design, and he sets it up on a miniature stage. Martha is almost always delighted. Noguchi is not practical in his stage designs——the set for *Seraphic Dialogue* would, he assured everyone concerned, fit into a big suitcase; it requires five crates, two to three days of polishing before each season, and some mechanical genius to erect——and neither is she. She seems to see with a single glance at the mock-up the impracticalities, the difficulties and obstacles the various pieces impose, the promising hazards she can put herself and the company through, and they are very challenging and satisfying. She rarely suggests changes; she will change her ideas instead. Once the design has been executed and delivered to the studio and she can drop the scavenged objects and work with the real thing, she may scrap parts of what she has done, develop and intensify other parts, and take off in a new direction. The final result is that the characters and the action are so directly and intimately related with the design that they give that sense of the *naturalness* of the whole.

Three weeks or so before the curtain is scheduled to go up, Jean Rosenthal telephones and shyly asks when she may be permitted to see the new works she must design the lighting for and when her stage manager, often someone new to the staff who does not know the repertory, may be permitted to come over with the cue-sheets and watch rehearsals. At about the same time, the conductor, Robert Irving these days, will call to ask when he may come to see the new works he must conduct. Martha resists. She is in the most difficult phase of the creative process, she is raw and vulnerable, and she has nothing but doubts about the new works. Everything is happening at once: she and the company are rehearsing the repertory from any hour of the morning far into the night; she is designing new costumes, redesigning old ones and supervising the making of them; she is being consulted about the countless details of theatrical production, salaries, billing, publicity, program notes, and the myriad other problems that will have come up.

"I'm being nibbled to death by ducks!"

In truth, she is out in the middle of the bog and running, exposed but thriving, and she does not want the stage manager's new face around or any strangers underfoot, and she is by no means ready to let Jean Rosenthal and Robert Irving see anything. No one from the world outside the School has seen the new works, not even the composers or Noguchi; only the accompanist, Eugene Lester, and the company and two or three members of the staff, whom she may on occasion invite

in, know about them. Eugene alone has seen her solos. She has made a kind of cone of privacy for herself and she is at the bottom, at the point of it, and she fights to stay there, knowing all the while that the time has come when the old conflict between the isolated creative artist and the director-performer must be resolved again. She knows full well that the new works must undergo a certain amount of preliminary exposure if they are ever to reach the stage, yet she has all of the artist's fears and uncertainties about exposing his creations. They are rough, unfinished; there are gaps; they are not good enough and perhaps never will be; failure is the evident possibility, even the likelihood.

"Why did I ever get myself into this? I never should have done it. I'll never do it again."

She cannot do it.

"Cancel the season."

After a number of Jean's shy requests, Martha gives in, allows the stage manager to lurk in a remote corner and watch rehearsals and schedules a run-through of the new works which Jean and Robert Irving may attend.

Jean's first direct encounter with Martha happened in the early thirties in a class at the Neighborhood Playhouse School of the Theatre. It was an encounter which killed whatever faint ambitions she might have had toward the art of dance.

"The only thing that could ever make you a dancer is that you've got peasant feet."

A few years later, when she had graduated from the Yale Drama School, Jean was managing Martha's stage and designing her lighting and their friendship and collaboration have continued unbroken ever since. There is between them the same empathy and understanding that exists between Martha and Noguchi and the same agreement about the aesthetics of the theater. No one but she ever lights Martha's plays and for a great many years she and her staff have been in charge of all technical matters.

The run-throughs are usually scheduled after nine at night or late on a Saturday or Sunday afternoon. Jean arrives. She and Martha may not have seen each other for a year or two, but their meeting is always the same, as if no time had intervened, even no time since they first worked together, for Jean's approach to Martha, her bearing, is still that of a student, humble, soft-spoken, in the presence of an adored master. A subtle change takes place in Martha: necessity accepted, with Jean at last on the premises, seated against the wall between the mirrors in the same position she herself has been occupying all these weeks and months, she gives way to the inevitability of performance. It is as though up to now there has been a dire uncertainty, a possibility that at the last moment nothing would ever get onto the stage. Jean's presence seems to banish uncertainty. She brings the stage and all its intricacies and technicalities with her and that is deeply reassuring. With her assistant and the stage manager, she sits quietly waiting. Robert Irving, a jolly ebullient Englishman who is nearly as reticent as Jean in Martha's presence, sits a discreet distance away, with his score ready on his knees.

The scene is chaotic. The studio is jammed with sets. The working area is reduced to half the space the play will require in performance. The

Jean Rosenthal, flanked by members of her staff, Robert Irving, and others in the studio

make-do objects are likely to be still in use. The dancers are in their motley garb, Martha in her usual black or some old costume that was handy and suggests what she will eventually wear. She sits on the floor facing Jean and talks about the play briefly, then she and the company go through it, or as much of it as may be "set," section by section, each of which by now has a name, usually poetic ("Silent Feast," for example). They start and stop; Martha bridges the gaps with sketchy descriptions. When the time comes for her solos, she substitutes airy comments:

"Now I do this little whoop-de-do."

Despite the chaos, the gaps and roughness, the garbs, the make-do objects, the structure of the play, whether or not it was originally set down in a script, is always immediately clear. It may be and most often is a very complex structure, but it strikes the eye and mind at once and it will rarely be deviated from, only embellished. Martha may revise a work over a period of years. *Night Journey,* first performed in 1947, underwent important revisions in its details as late as 1954. The Epilogue of *Clytemnestra* was completely changed between its first and second seasons. Owing to the necessity to replace a dancer, the Warrior section of *Seraphic Dialogue* was re-choreographed in a hotel banquet-room in New Delhi and changed from a solo to a duet for Joan and St. Michael Between its run-throughs in the studio and its premiere at the Habimah Theatre in Tel Aviv, *Legend of Judith* underwent all kinds of alterations. In each case, however, the original structure of the work, the shape of the seashell, so to speak, held firm. Once embellished to her satisfaction, the play in all its details is as fixed as though it were in print. She is never really satisfied, but she is shrewd enough to know when she is in the vicinity of perfection and to let well enough alone, and well enough for her means primarily a rightness of dramatic structure, a certainty that the play could not possibly have been built in any other way.

At the circus, it hardly matters whether the trained seals come before the juggler or the lion tamer before the high-wire artist; in *Acrobats of*

God, the acts and star turns cannot be shuffled, for each comes precisely when and where it must to assure the total effect.

When the curtain rises on *Seraphic Dialogue,* Joan of Arc is seated, in an attitude both humble and withdrawn, below the façade of what is at once Heaven and some place of ultimate inner illumination. Her saints are behind the façade and St. Michael's hand is high, fluttering, as if it were the Holy Spirit as the Dove. Like Tiresias in *Night Journey,* he, or that part of Joan which guided her destiny, causes the action: Martha keeps insisting that there is something in the being which demands illumination, the "something" which makes it impossible for movement to lie. The action takes place outside of time, in the limbo following Joan's death at the stake. She rises and the Maid, the Warrior, and the Martyr enter in stately ceremonial file in regal capes, blue, rich dark green, scarlet, and from their entrance, as the action alternates between Joan's solos and the dialogues with her other selves, the feeling is of a *rite de passage,* noble with age, stark in its simplicity, opulent in its beauty, always enacted in this and no other possible way.

Like *Seraphic Dialogue,* Martha's best works are always models of poetic density, economy, and compression. She can convey more in twenty-five minutes than most playwrights can manage to do in three acts. They are also ideal examples of a uniquely modern mind, revolutionary but conservative, deeply traditional but free as the wind, responding to myths, legends, and history, to what is "worthy to be remembered" in human experience and demonstrating its adaptability and truth

in the present. There is no guessing beforehand how that mind will respond; how, as she works, with her sources, finding shapes of her inner landscape in them, she will remold them. It is certain that the originality of her insight and of her approach will surprise and startle; that she will dismiss time and take full liberty with the events of an action and with the facts. She will cause things to happen out of familiar sequence and in ways and under conditions contrary to the known, but she never violates her source and never debases it. In fact, she elevates her protagonists by bestowing upon them depths of feeling and emotion and a richer humanity than they had ever been imagined to possess. Martha's Jocasta in *Night Journey* is characterized by a queenliness of stature and an intensity of love and passion of which there is little or no hint in *Oedipus Rex.* The play is guided and shaped by these qualities and the point of view is Jocasta's throughout. When, forced by Tiresias, she is ready fully to confront the tragedy, Oedipus is led in by the chorus of "Daughters of the Night." Fresh from his encounter with the Sphinx, heroic and arrogant, he climbs to the bed where Jocasta lies—it is as though he climbs up out of the dark of her memory—and lifts her and carries her high on his shoulder, a prize won but not yet possessed, into the action proper, directly into the region of the mind where the instant and the past that is not past collide. A courtship dance follows which is an archetype of all courting of women by men and men by women: they seduce, win, and possess each other, moving through the broad spectrum of emotions that are aroused in the process, through the unavoidable abrasions of personality, submission of wills, quelling of force and of fear and the awakening of love. It all takes place in what is at once their first meeting and first night and all the nights they ever spent together and it ends when they ensnare each other with the rope whose meaning they do not know until Tiresias reappears to break it.

The elevation of Jocasta to protagonist, the departure in point of view, the remarkable compression of events, were innovation enough, but Martha had another to offer: the Daughters of the Night. She had used the chorus as a dramatic instrument earlier in *Cave of the Heart,* but concentrated its function in a single compassionate character, derived from Medea's Nurse, who foresees and tries to avert the course of events and who serves as a medium through which the spectator observes and suffers the action. She has used the chorus since, in *Clytemnestra,* but only as an embellishment. In *Night Journey* she fully restored it as it was used in Greek drama to the modern theater. The Daughters of the Night are six, sometimes more; they move in unison through a series of dances that are in a very real sense speeches of a poetic depth and grandeur comparable with any found in classical Greek drama. Their role in the play is as integral as Tiresias's; their foreknowledge is equivalent to his; their compassion provides the catharsis.

Neither to the Greeks nor to anyone else did it ever occur to try to redeem Clytemnestra or to imagine that she might want to be redeemed. But it must be that she did; that, in Jungian terms, she, as an archetype, has been lodged in the collective unconscious ever since Aeschylus consigned her to the Underworld, waiting for the right poet to come down and bring her out to a place of honor. Martha, finding her there, knew her at once, for Clytemnestra, in the complexity of her character, had marked affinities with a number of her own heroines and the people and events of Clytemnestra's life and time were rife with her own abiding preoccupations. Like Medea, she was violent, implacable in revenge, an exultant murderess, and, through the Furies, a sorceress with some control of the world's dark powers. Like Jocasta she was in a sense an innocent victim: if the house of Mycenae had not been under a curse in the first place; if she had not been Helen's unfavored twin and if Helen and Paris had not met; if the winds had not been stilled at Aulis; if the Trojan War had not taken place; if she had not been left alone to rule the kingdom, she might have behaved differently. As a wife, she might once have been faithful and loving. As a woman, she was, like Phaedra, governed by lust. As a queen, she was, like Mary Stuart, ruthless and avid for power. As a mother, she loved Iphigenia, the Sacrificial Virgin, above all others. In Clytemnestra, Martha saw concentrated the leit-motifs of her creative life.

The curtain rises on a Clytemnestra who is consumed with righteous indignation, defiant of King Hades, demanding honor. The long Prologue is an orgy of self-justification and, as Martha has devised it, a brilliant reversal of the *Oresteia,* for she turns the Underworld into something like a court of law. Apollo and Athena are brought down but they do not preside. It is Clytemnestra's court and she summons her arguments for the guilt of others: Helen's guilt as she paces the battlements of Troy, led by Athena and as though compelled by her to look down upon the rape of the town; Agamemnon's, as he sacrifices Iphigenia at Aulis; Orestes's and Electra's, as they meet and plot Clytemnestra's murder. The argument and the self-justification are brought to a high sustained pitch when the central characters reappear and others are introduced and Clytemnestra and Orestes encounter them in juxtaposition: she and Helen, he and Paris, she and Electra, he and Aegisthus, she and Iphigenia, he and Agamemnon, finally she and Cassandra, in an order subtly devised to bring Clytemnestra to a peak of rage and only then is it clear that the process in this court of law has been headed toward further violence, that the time of the action has been prior to Clytemnestra's revenge against Orestes, that she has presented her arguments to justify herself in letting the Furies loose upon him.

Act I takes place on earth and begins as the *Oresteia* does with the Watchman announcing the end of the war and the return of Agamemnon. Clytemnestra appears alone. The point of view remains hers and she is still in the midst of her last act of violence, the Furies are out there somewhere hounding Orestes, but with the movement backward in time and the consequent loss of knowledge, there is a marked change in her. She is watching herself as she was, as in part she still is, and this watching, growing more and more intense, moves the theme forward to its resolution. Swathed in a long purple veil which signifies her regal position, her mourning for Iphigenia and, perhaps, her immediate mourning for what in the past she is about to do, she stands briefly, raging but indecisive, lost in the emptiness of the soul which comes before the commitment to evil. Martha conveys this in an instant by the way she stands and the way she moves. After a barbaric dance of celebration by the women of Mycenae, Clytemnestra plunges into her long "meditation," the earlier phase of her self-justification, and the mood as the gates of the past open and close is curiously quiet, as though, at next to the last moment of decision, the argument may be hushed. She sees herself and Aegisthus in their abandoned relationship, seeing him clearly as a tempting but pompous weakling whose only strength is in his whip. She sees Helen seduced by Paris in a poignant vision which, following directly upon the first, is almost wishful, as though she would have chosen to be Helen and to have had her fate. Finally, she sees again the ritual sacrifice of Iphigenia and this prepares her for her decisive meeting with Aegisthus. She is still not quite ready for murder. He makes her ready by making love to her, arousing her lust while forcing her hand onto a dagger of exaggerated size, overcoming her last frail qualms. From this point on, Act I follows the *Oresteia* fairly closely but under extreme compression and with certain innovations: after the murder of Agememnon and Cassandra, Helen appears to lament the unceasing violence and to confront a Clytemnestra now wholly evil; a depraved dance of triumph by Aegisthus and Clytemnestra; and, as the curtain falls, the sudden doomful appearance of the Messenger of Death.

Act II, set in the royal bedchamber of the palace at Mycenae, is Clytemnestra's nightmare, both dream and reality, during which the ghost of

Agamemnon demands revenge and Orestes and Electra again meet and plot her murder. The four of them come together in a quadrille that Martha calls "Family Portrait": chillingly Gothic, it sums up everything she has ever had to say about the black side of blood relationships. The act ends with the murder of Clytemnestra and Aegisthus and with the unleashing again of the Furies. Structurally, the long Prologue is reduced at a stroke to an instant.

The Epilogue takes place in a transformed Underworld. It has become a place of light. Hades is present, Apollo and Athena preside, but it is Clytemnestra who has redeemed herself. She embraces Orestes with the love she has reserved hitherto only for Iphigenia, turns her own Furies into the Eumenides, takes from Hades the black leaves that have been the symbol of his power and goes away alone with honor.

Martha is as free in her dealings with historical personages as she is with those of myth. Often she ignores dominant traits of character, explores others little noticed and builds her play upon them. Mary Stuart's treachery against Elizabeth for the throne of England did not interest her. She condensed the power politics into an elegant tennis match played between the two Queens while in the background, against a massive scaffold, the black-clad ladies and gentlemen of the court performed an austerely beautiful dance of mourning. When Mary Stuart lost, watched the non-existent ball fly past her and away, one saw all of England

go out of her grasp. What did interest Martha was the passionate woman who happened to be the Roman Catholic Queen and the peculiar courage she poured into the staging of her execution, the fact that she made of it an act of theater, designed her own costume and those of her ladies as though for her coronation and went so far in consideration of the spectators as to wear an undress of scarlet so that, when the blood flowed, it would be less shocking to the eye. Such an "imperial gesture"— she did a work with that title in 1935—not bigger than life but as big as life may sometimes be made to be, dictated by an inviolate image of one's self and one's relations with the phenomenal world and projected into that world with the force and directness that come from having stood stiffly against the inward and outward terrors, has always fascinated Martha, even obsessed her and it helps account for some of her power as a dramatist and an actress. Her protagonists are caught in the midst of an imperial gesture in relation not with the world and men but with themselves and Martha as she plays them makes an imperial gesture of it.

The three weeks or so before opening night are full of Mack Sennett activity. Serious, efficient, it has the old-movie, stepped-up frenzy because it is all being done on a shoestring. Martha has been as close to bankruptcy as anyone can get throughout most of her creative life. Until she received the munificent Aspen award in 1965, she had never had any money of her own and she owned nothing but her wardrobe, extensive and fine but not at all what would be expected for a woman of her fame, some jewelry, the furniture and books in her apartment, and an excellent random collection of art objects, mostly Oriental, most of which has been given to her. Until the National Council on the Arts gave her a grant in 1966, she had never had a substantial sum to put into new productions or to underwrite the losses of an American tour. In place of money, she has an attitude toward it:

"Money? Money's nothing. If we *need* it, we'll have it."

She elevates economics to the realm of spirit. The surest way to set her thinking about a shopping spree is to tell her she is overdrawn at the bank. She is convinced that the time to spend money is the time when you have none, for in that way you affirm God's inexhaustible bounty. If she hears that someone close to her is broke, she will lend or give large amounts.

"I'll just take out a loan at the bank . . . they're dying to lend me money."

Her faith in money matters has been unshakeable and justified. When she *needs* money, she always does somehow get it. Ever since 1926, when Miss Frances Steloff of the Gotham Book Mart borrowed a thousand dollars for her to cover the costs of that first historical appearance at the 48th Street Theatre, Martha has had friends to help her do what she needed to do, either with money—usually, in theatrical terms, very small sums; even now, the costs of her theater, compared with the costs of ballet productions, are minuscule—or with time and work. There seems always to have been someone like Miss Steloff or Katharine Cornell or, since 1950, Bethsabee de Rothschild, who has been convinced of her greatness and who was able and willing to give financial

support. There have always been others with the same conviction, like Jean Rosenthal, Isadora Bennett, the press agent, Gertrude Macy, the producer, who were willing to work day and night for next to nothing or for nothing at all to bring her to the stage. The loyalties she inspires are awesome. She deserves them. No one who has given her money, energy, or time seems ever to have regretted it: the selflessness with which they gave and still give is perhaps the opposite, for there is something remarkably self-fulfilling in being involved in whatever way with Martha herself, with her creative processes, and with her theater. One rarely has the opportunity to be caught up in life being lived at full pitch on a shoe string.

Owing to Bethsabee de Rothschild's support, and in 1966 to the Federal Government, Mrs. DeWitt Wallace and others, it has been in recent years a fairly thick and sturdy string; nevertheless, and despite Martha's spiritual economics, it is one. Everyone including Martha works for very little and some for nothing. Everyone, and especially the company, is crazily overworked and that enhances the Mack Sennett atmosphere.

In addition to Georgia Sargeant, Martha's sister, who is the registrar of the School, there is a permanent staff of two and they are not Martha's employees. Craig Barton, who acts as her manager and personal representative, is the director of the B. de Rothschild Foundation, a full-time job itself. Jessica Colfer, who handles much of her correspondence, pays her bills, worries about her bank imbalances, and does a great deal of clerical and administrative work for the School and the theatrical productions, is the executive secretary of the Foundation, also a full-time job. During performance periods, a third person is usually added to do the work these two are unable to handle, and a fourth, outside, to act as producer. Six, eight, or ten others, or, on occasion, anyone caught looking idle, scurry on countless errands and do countless odd jobs.

Irritants delightfully abound now. A dancer, dissatisfied with the salary, sulks. Another, dissatisfied with a role, is truculent. Another, estranged through the mysterious processes of creativity, hovers like a ghost and a constant reproach. Others harp on the new works. They are sceptical, for nothing is finished and probably nothing will be. They say they do not know what they're supposed to be doing and they think Martha doesn't know either. Minutes before the premiere of *Embattled Garden,* the Stranger vomited in his dressing room because he did not know what the play was about. Like any other artist, on occasion and contrary to her usual working methods, Martha has gone blind into a new work and had to fumble her way, the company following. This was the case with *Embattled Garden.* It is remarkable that she found her way through it, for she was doing *Clytemnestra* at the same time. It is more remarkable that, at its premiere, the play was finished, perfectly polished and clear, and has never been changed, even in the smallest detail. However, caught in the throes, the dancers cannot count on this; her vision, eluding her, eludes them also, of course. Consequently, she spends all of her time on the new works, refusing to rehearse the repertory, but then, they say, she won't let well enough alone; she does a beautiful sequence one day and throws it out the next. But she:

"I haven't had a minute to work on myself. Clear the building. Get the company out of here, they've rehearsed enough. I've got to have some time alone."

True: her survival as an artist depends upon it, especially at this critical juncture when the new works, no matter what Jean Rosenthal might have seen in them at the run-throughs, are most slippery and keep slithering away out of her grasp headed for certain failure. The company goes, but then a horde of students comes and they must be allowed in and they cannot be kept quiet in the hallways as they wait to get into the studio where Martha is trying to have time to herself and they cannot be taught to use ashtrays instead of the waxed floors or be prevented from leaving sweaty leotards and tights in the dressing rooms or from peeking through the crack at the studio door. Though they have been erring in these ways all year, it will not be tolerated now.

Martha's way of exit from the studio to what used to be her private dressing room leads her through the kitchen. Small as it is and inconveniently shaped like a truncated L, it is, during this period, with everything that is going on in the other parts of the building, the only gathering place for the company and it is always a shambles. No one is ever assigned to K. P. duty. Seething, slamming doors, uttering withering curses, Martha does it, while her lunch or some nameless meal cooks.

Her eating habits are not as eccentric as they used to be, but they are still interesting and unpredictable. She used to say she did not have time to think about food and, besides, it is better al-

ways to eat the same thing. Once, for many weeks, she ate nothing for lunch but boiled ham and swiss cheese. During another period, and for months it seemed, she ate nothing but canned hamburgers, and then, for an even longer time, a variation on egg-drop soup that she made by swirling raw beaten eggs into boiling beef stock very heavily flavored with garlic powder. She was once a vegetarian, but then her doctor told her she must have the nourishment meat gives and she ate steak every day. She never drinks water: "It makes you fat. Besides, it makes you sweat." Whatever her diet, it has kept her very slim and in invincible good health. She went to a hospital as a patient for the first time in her life in 1965 for a hernia operation. In the groin, the hernia was massive, but she had been putting up with it, and dancing in spite of it, for more than twenty years.

Past the kitchen, in the all-purpose space that used to be her dressing room, someone will be "lurking, ready to pounce": Craig Barton, with a sheaf of problems and the week's unanswered questions; Jessica Colfer, with the problems and questions of her domain; Georgia Sargeant with hers. Martha:

"I cannot think about that now."

One of Craig Barton's problems is sure to be that the new works have no titles. The announcement of the premiere of an "Untitled New Work" is so customary in Martha's advance publicity—customary, in fact, in the advance publicity of many dance companies, as if it is a vogue Martha started long ago—that Bertram Ross as choreographer has in his repertory a work called *Untitled*. Martha does not deliberately withhold the information; she is simply reluctant to put a tag on until the work is finished. She likes poetic titles and for quite a long time now she has wanted, for each new work, to get the word "God" in somewhere; her repertory threatened to sound exclusively, fervently evangelical. Craig Barton, his printers and ad men waited until the last possible minute before a title as straightforward as *Clytemnestra* or *Alcestis* or *Phaedra* or *The Witch of Endor* could be announced.

Another of his problems is sure to be the press and the photographers. Martha's innate shyness, her uncertainty in public, her dislike of speaking about herself has kept her all but inaccessible to the press throughout most of her creative life. Much as she has been photographed, she still loathes the camera. As late as 1954, considerable courage was required even to broach to her the possibility of a press interview; photographers were unmentionable. That year however, making her first tour of Europe with her company, she began to give way a little and, in 1955-1956, when she and the company toured the Orient as "cultural ambassadors" for the State Department, she gave in completely. The first stop, Japan, that land of amateur photographers and *Front Page* reporters, left her no choice; in fact, the mission left her no choice. She accepted it fully and made herself available upon request to newsmen, photographers, the radio, and public occasions of many kinds, including Rotary Club luncheons, in a display of stamina reminiscent of Eleanor Roosevelt's, but not even Mrs. Roosevelt was required, after such scheduled days, to perform on stage. Dislike them though she still does, resist them though she still does in America, going in to them like a reluctant snake charmer, Martha is masterful in newspaper and radio interviews and press conferences and the reporter is rare who is not brought to his knees by her. She is masterful, too, when she lectures. She does it seldom and grudgingly, always extemporaneously and with a certain amount of illogic, but that scarcely matters; her quality seduces and it is in her voice. It is a most unusual sound: devoid of the narcissism of the orator, the calculations of the actor, the causes of the politician and persuader, the biases of the preacher, it is a kind of music which wells up out of an achieved wholeness of the personality, its measures shaped by a lifetime of integrity and impassioned conviction in the practice of an art.

Past the gamut of problems and questions—set aside for the time being—in the front studio, now made all but impassable by crates and sets and work tables and costume racks, Ursula Reed, jammed into a corner, justifiably smolders. She has the entire wardrobe on her hands; she is worked beyond endurance; her patience and natural good temper have long since been worn to shreds. Martha designs the costumes. At this late date, there is likely to be a whole set of them she has not yet put her mind to; the designing of her own she usually leaves to the last. She may not even have selected fabrics, but it does no good to try to force samples and swatches upon her.

"Don't push me."

Like most stage sets, most theatrical costumes are dramatically inert: they are right if they are right for the period and the character, rags for the beggar, something gaudy for the loose woman; dictated by the character's station in life and the current vogue, they signify little else. Martha's costumes, like the other elements of her theater, are entirely original and an integral part of the total effect. There is nothing like them to be seen on any other stage and there is no one in the theater who uses them as she does for dramatic purposes. She puts costumes to work. Fundamental to her approach is the old sense of the significance of dress, of dressing as ritualistic change, of the poetic meaning inherent in the "putting on of garments," that sense which has, except in the rare coronation, in certain rites of the churches, in the bride's white gown that she will wear once and never again, in the boy's short pants suddenly changed one day for long, all but vanished from the modern mind. It permeates Martha's plays. Her characters, in particular those she portrays, are often ritually dressed in the course of the action or they shed outer garments to convey changes not of worldly status but of states of mind and heart. In *Episodes,* she wanted but did not get, since she did not design the costumes herself, a costume for Mary Stuart which would have conveyed at first sight the theme of the play. It was to have been a fair copy of an Elizabethan court dress, but transparent, all of its ribs and braces visible, like a cage inside of which one could see the slight trapped body of a woman. When she released herself from it, it was to stand on a landing leading to the scaffold, a regal shell to dominate the action.

At their simplest, Martha's costumes are designed for the movement she has devised. When she takes a sample of fabric between her fingers, she seems to feel for its capacity not only to mold the body and reveal and emphasize the beauty of its contours but to conduct energy. It must promise to show the body's dynamic impulses and carry them visibly through. When the play permits, she clothes her dancers in as little as possible, the men in the briefest trunks, the women in the tightest adaptations of the leotard. Her skirts and dresses are usually made of silk jersey, to which she is partial. Unfortunately, it stretches in length as it hangs and one of the most familiar sights backstage before curtain time is the sight of Martha and the other dancers trimming inches off their skirts.

Her more complex and dramatically more meaningful costumes are designed against the movement. She has put herself and her dancers into tubes of cloth like cocoons; in voluminous robes, weighty and unyielding; in cloaks and capes made of yards of material and so intricately designed, tacked, hooked-and-eyed that the dancers forget from one season to the next how to put them on. In short, she often designs obstacles she and the dancers must overcome while they are also overcoming the obstacles posed by the set and by the movement itself and the latter would be difficult enough if they wore nothing at all. Often, she works on the risky but, for her, quite safe principle of exaggeration for dramatic and poetic effect. The cape Clytemnestra offers Agamemnon conveys by its very length the magnitude of her vengefulness; pulled taut, lying to his gaze, it seems to cover the kingdom of Mycenae like an impenetrable fog. Tiresias's robe in *Night Journey* is very heavy, cumbersome, and exaggerated in length. It hampers him and he struggles against it as it whips around him and drags after him; it projects his torment and he would be a less powerful figure dressed in another way. The capes the Maid, the Warrior, and the Martyr wear in *Seraphic Dialogue* are also very heavy and long; when these three figures first file into view, the immediate impression is of the weight of destiny upon the frail being elected to bear it. As the Maid and the Warrior rise in turn to enact their phases of that destiny, their capes are used to cover Joan the protagonist, like shells of the living past she withdraws into. When the Martyr rises, her cape is used to conceal Joan; from behind it, she vanishes from the stage, as though in the act of reliving the martyrdom spirit and flesh again become one.

Martha is partial to capes. Oedipus wears one designed like a Chinese puzzle and he moves in it and handles it in ways that render it symbolic of his manhood, his heroism, and his authority. At the climax of the courtship dance, he covers Jocasta with it and they become at once king and consort, man and wife. Agamemnon's proper cape is narrow, elongated, and, ironically, made of simulated tiger skin. When, to reclaim Clytemnestra as his wife, he covers her with it, she throws it rudely off; later, he sends it flying across the stage to coil around Cassandra's feet in a defiant gesture of possession. In *The Witch of Endor,* the witch has an enormous, magnificent black-red-and-gold cape she puts on to give her the power to summon the ghost of the prophet, Samuel.

Despite this partiality and another for veils and another for yards of cloth which, in her hands, seem to come to life, Martha is as unpredictable in her costuming as she is in all else. The cast of characters and the action of *Clytemnestra* offered the opportunity for a rich variety of dress and changes of dress. Martha passed it by: everyone, including Clytemnestra, wears the same costume throughout and all of the women except Cassandra wear black. Dramatically, it is dead right. The high moment in Judith's story, when she takes off her mourning garments and puts on her finery to delight and seduce Holofernes, offered another. Martha could have made a great deal out of it, but she chose to use a length of silvery cloth and to drape it like a cape about her. After the murder, it serves as a strange field for Holofernes's severed head, making a shocking vision that would be Grand Guignol, a mere *coup de théâtre,* if the cloth did not by then bear a wealth of poetic meaning.

Costumes unfinished, new works unfinished, questions unanswered, problems unsolved: when the day comes for the move into the theater, scarcely anything seems to be ready but the bog and Martha is far out in it and the more it threatens to pull her under, the readier she gets. "Don't push me" really means push harder, put more pressure on, heighten the tension, for only the last minute is the right minute.

The move into the theater necessitates even more stringent economies and wears the shoestring thin. One of the quirks that govern Broadway operations is that no distinction is made between a production with commercial aims and one that has none. Martha's theater moves onto Broadway under the same rules, regulations, and high costs as those of a hopeful musical comedy; no concessions are made to the fact that her engagement will last a maximum of three weeks and must, therefore, even with sold-out houses, close with a deficit of many thousands of dollars. So everything but union wages and union man-hours is cut to the bone. Years ago, faced with the costs of rehearsing an orchestra and maintaining it, Martha set a pattern of commissioning new scores that required no more than twenty to twenty-two players. The extraordinary body of music she has caused to be written is exclusively for chamber orchestra. Difficult, demanding music, the best musicians in the city must be hired if it is to be mastered in the brief rehearsal time the budget allows. The dancers rarely have the opportunity to rehearse any of the works, including the new, with this orchestra more than once. They never have a dress rehearsal, complete with orchestra, sets, lights, and costumes, because that costs as much as a performance for a paid audience. They are allowed a lighting rehearsal with Jean Rosenthal, a session called a "piano-dress" with such costumes as are ready and with the set, and a rehearsal with the orchestra and set but no lights. The rest of the time, if there is any, they must work in practice clothes on a bare stage in the stark chiaroscuro cast by the work light, a single powerful naked bulb. Under these conditions, if it were not for their high professionalism, their single-mindedness and purposefulness, and, no doubt for the fact that they have never known easier working conditions, the curtain would never go up.

Once in the theater, Martha seems to be at home in a way that she never is elsewhere. Her dressing room, the stage, the auditorium, empty

or packed, are for her what a house, great or small, is for a lady: her domain, her rightful place. No matter how luxurious or how crude—she has dressed in tents and in lean-tos with dirt floors—the theater is hers and she moves through it with the grace and decorum of a fine hostess giving the best party of the year. Irritants abound still and there are occasions for rage, but most of the time her voice is soft and it is as though she has arrived at some serene place in her inner landscape. Working with Jean Rosenthal, with Robert Irving, she is docile; she puts herself and the work in their hands. It is very rare that she has an objection to Jean's lighting or to Mr. Irving's interpretation of the music. She may feel that the stage is a little too dark or that a passage of music is being taken a little too fast or slow, but her remarks take the form of shy questions. With the stagehands, the doorman, the wardrobe mistress, her manners are impeccable and warm. The same is generally true of the company. Together, they create backstage an atmosphere that is, to say the least, unusual.

As they rehearse, even on a bare stage with nothing but the work light and the muffled accompaniment of the piano, Martha and the best of the company undergo a fascinating and richly instructive change. At the first note of the music, their gazes turn inward and they seem to move into a state of luminous introspection and to be unaware that any world exists beyond the proscenium arch. In truth, they are intensely aware: their hearing is doubly sharp, they are hypersensitive to the subtleties of an audience's mood and they chatter about it· and many another thing under their breath while they perform, but no one would ever know that. From the audience, the proscenium arch suddenly seems to be a frame for the clearest pane of glass through which one is secretly privileged to watch an action which has never happened before and will never happen again; which, though it is happening only because the spectator is there, seems to ignore his existence, for it never makes a direct appeal to him, never caters to his taste or expectations, simply allows him, if he is so inclined, to be a witness, and, if he is capable, to be moved. Few dramatists, very few actors, achieve this independence of and intimate relationship with their audience.

The choreographing, revising, the costume designing and making, the rehearsing, the scurrying around town go on until curtain time on opening night and for days afterwards. In the midst of an epidemic of exhaustion and frazzled nerves, there is a steady surge of vitality. Before an opening, Martha is likely to have worked most of the night and on through the day and she arrives at the theater haggard. She prefers to be in her dressing room two hours or so before curtain time, for it is there that she sheds her fatigue. She brings talismans for her dressing table: a bronze dancing Shiva, a Chinese or Greek figurine, a piece of carved jade she holds tight in her fist; they comfort her. She brings books: the Bible, poetry, a murder mystery, a scholarly work on some arcane subject. She has her notebooks on the repertory and studies them. She rests in the gloom. She putters. She checks on the company to be sure that they are on time and all right. She frets about tickets she has reserved for the grocer, the maid,

a random cab driver, old friends. She never asks about the box-office receipts or advance sales and she would rather not know about celebrities in the audience. She spends a long time on her make-up and her hair, makes last minute changes in her costume, trims the hem. Using a chair for a barre, she warms up.

Going to the stage, she goes toward what is for her the true vibrant center of the microcosm she has brought into being. At that other center, in the studio, in the gloom, being the willing instrument, driven to discover for herself the laws of her art, she was in her own eyes a drudge; now she is ready for the conquering. On stage, she stands almost hidden in a dark wing, surrounded by a space of quiet. Move into it to wish her luck and her thanks come in a whisper. She may offer her hand, but she is remote, withdrawn into her Venus-shell, alert for the cue and the wash of light to bring her out to be Clytemnestra or Phaedra or Alcestis or Jocasta or the Witch of Endor or Judith, who, old, doubts glory and the good of conquering, or the comical, but most moving and understandable artist in *Acrobats of God.*

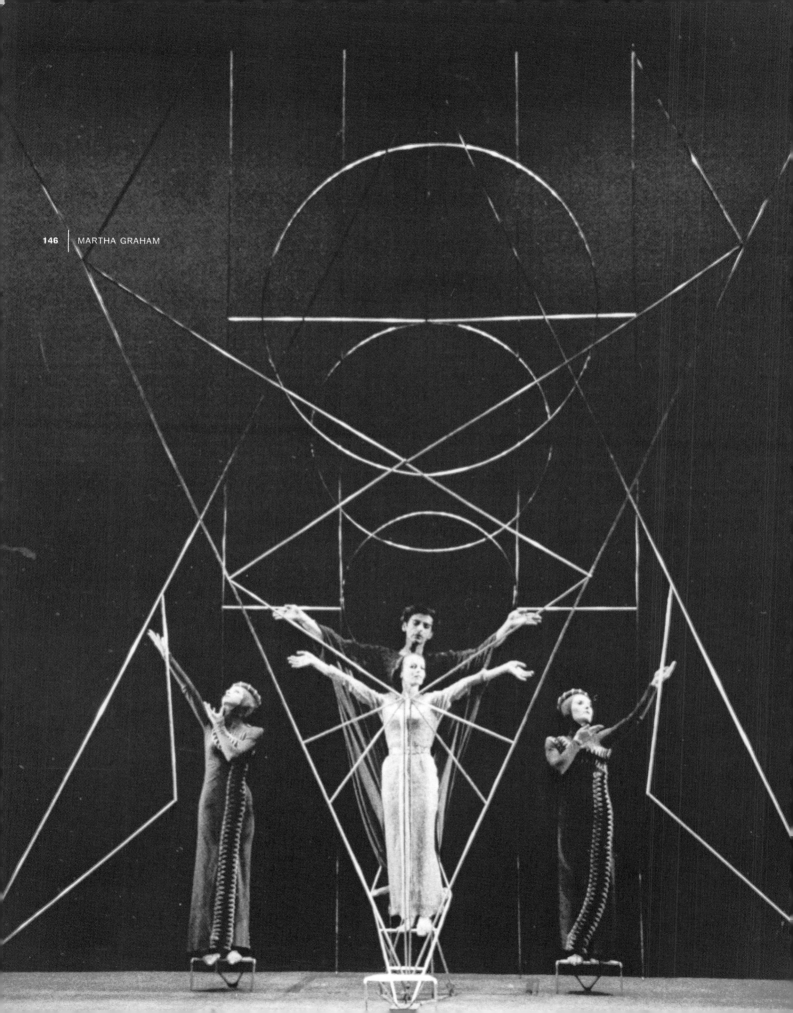

SERAPHIC DIALOGUE

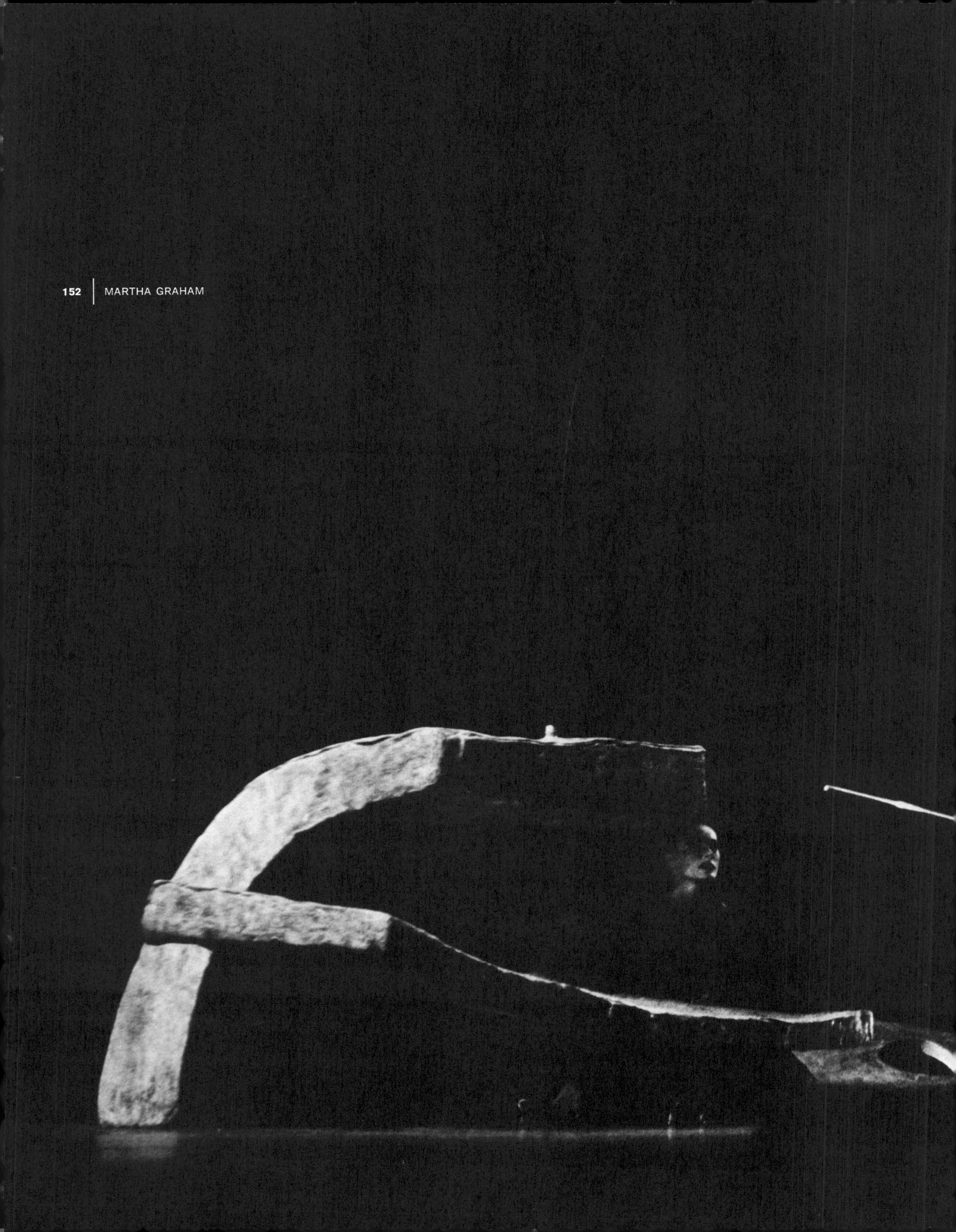

LEGEND OF JUDITH

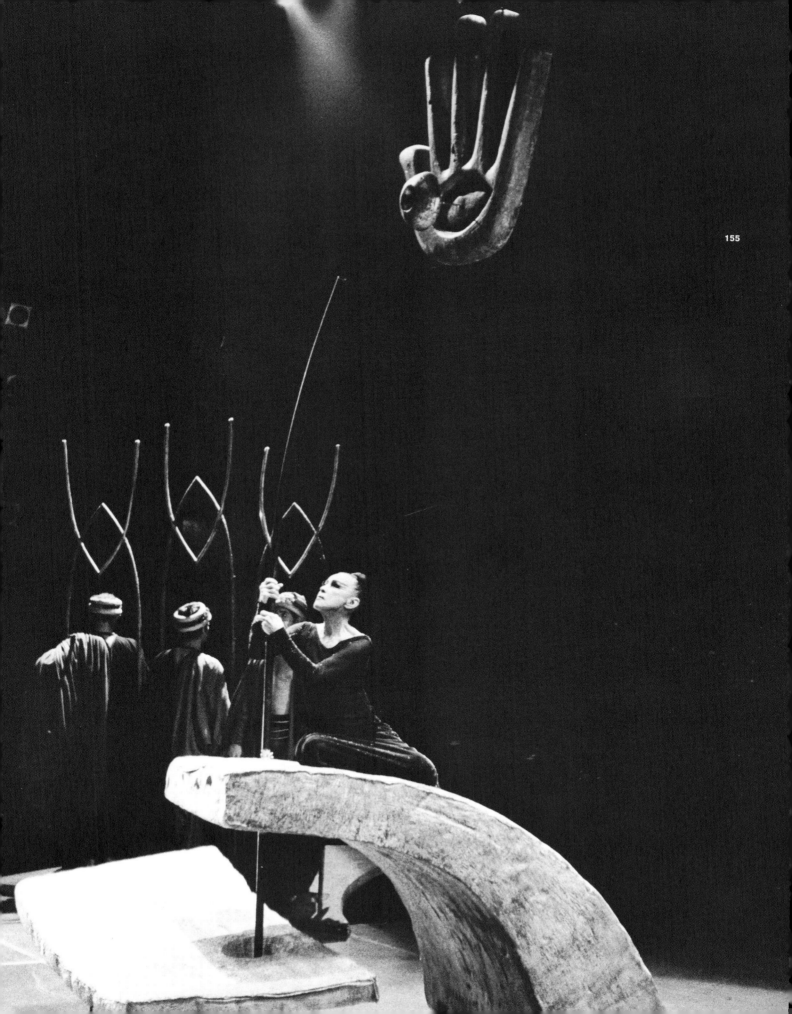

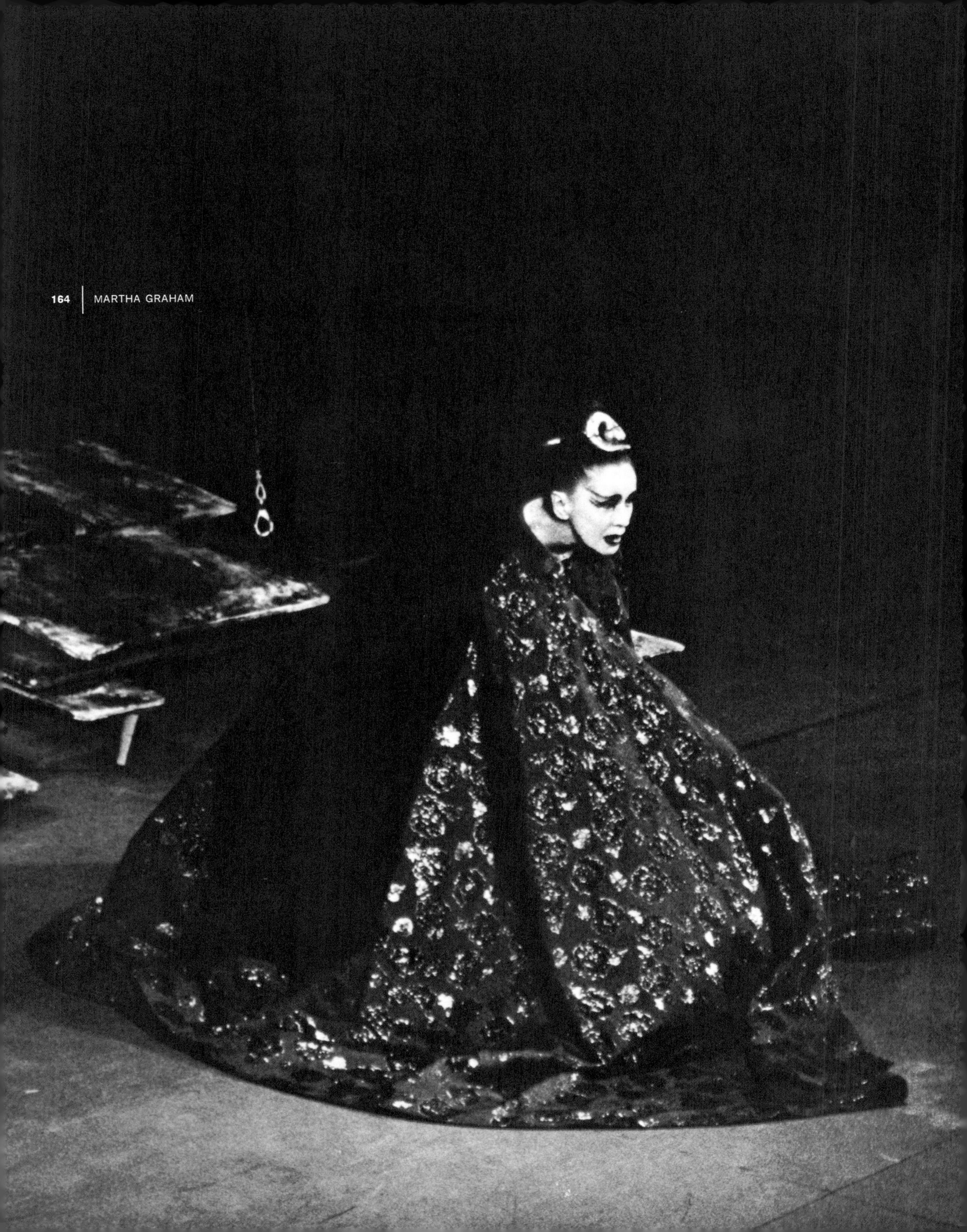

THE WITCH OF ENDOR

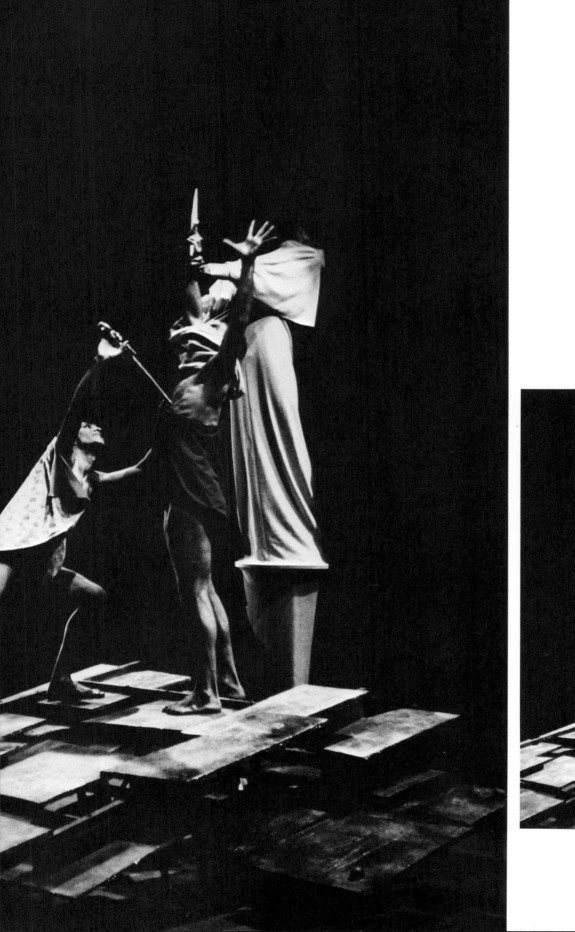

APPENDIX

Complete Chronological List of Dances Composed by Martha Graham
from April 1926 to November 1965, as Compiled by Louis Horst, Robert Sabin,
and LeRoy Leatherman

Except where noted, all costumes were designed by Miss Graham.

1
CHORALE
Music by César Franck
Première: April 18, 1926

2
NOVELETTE
Music by William Schuman
Première: April 18, 1926

3
TANZE
Music by Franz Schubert
Première: April 18, 1926

4
INTERMEZZO
Music by Johannes Brahms
Première: April 18, 1926

5
MAID WITH FLAXEN HAIR
Music by Claude Debussy
Première: April 18, 1926

6
ARABESQUE
Music by Claude Debussy
Première: April 18, 1926

7
CLAIR DE LUNE
Music by Claude Debussy
Première: April 18, 1926

8
DANSE LANGUIDE
Music by Aleksandr Scriabin
Première: April 18, 1926

9
DESIR
Music by Aleksandr Scriabin
Première: April 18, 1926

10
DEUX VALSES SENTIMENTALES
Music by Maurice Ravel
Première: April 18, 1926

11
TANAGRA
Music by Erik Satie
Première: April 18, 1926

12
A FLORENTINE MADONNA
Music by Sergei Rachmaninoff
Première: April 18, 1926

13
GNOSSIENNE
Music by Erik Satie
Première: April 18, 1926

14
A STUDY IN LACQUER
Music by Marcel Bernheim
Première: April 18, 1926

15
THREE GOPI MAIDENS
Music by Cyril Scott
Première: April 18, 1926

16
DANSE ROCOCO
Music by Maurice Ravel
Première: April 18, 1926

17
MARIONETTE SHOW
Music by Eugene Goossens
Première: April 18, 1926

18
GYPSY PORTRAIT
Music by Manuel de Falla
Première: April 18, 1926

19
ANGELI
Music by Ermanno Wolf-Ferrari
Première: May 27, 1926

20
PRELUDE FROM "ALCESTE"
Music by Christoph Willibald von Gluck
Première: May 27, 1926

21
SCHERZO
Music by Felix Mendelssohn
Première: November 28, 1926

22
BAAL SHEM
Music by Ernest Bloch
Première: November 28, 1926

23
THE MOTH
Music by Claude Debussy
Première: November 28, 1926

24
ALT-WIEN
Music arranged by Louis Horst
Première: November 28, 1926

25
THREE POEMS OF THE EAST
Music by Louis Horst
Première: November 28, 1926

26
PEASANT SKETCHES
1. Dance
Music by Vladimir Rebikov
2. Berceuse
Music by Alexander Tansman
3. In the Church
Music by Peter Tschaikovsky
Première: February 27, 1927

27
TUNISIA
Music by Ede Poldini
Première: February 27, 1927

28
LUCREZIA
Music by Claude Debussy
Première: February 27, 1927

29
LA CANCION
Music by René Defossez
Première: February 27, 1927

30
SPIRES
Music by Johann Sebastian Bach
Première: October 16, 1927

31
MADONNA
Music by George Frideric Handel
Première: October 16, 1927

32
FRAGILITE
Music by Aleksandr Scriabin
Première: October 16, 1927

33
LUGUBRE
Music by Aleksandr Scriabin
Première: October 16, 1927

34
POEME AILE
Music by Aleksandr Scriabin
Première: October 16, 1927

35
TANZSTUCK
Music by Paul Hindemith
Première: October 16, 1927

36
REVOLT
Music by Arthur Honegger
Première: October 16, 1927

37
ESQUISSE ANTIQUE
Music by Desiré Inghelbrecht
Première: October 16, 1927

38
RONDE
Music by Rhené-Baton
Première: October 16, 1927

39
VALSE NOBLE
Music by Maurice Ravel
Première: April 22, 1928

40
TROUVERES
Music by Charles Koechlin
Première: April 22, 1928

41
IMMIGRANT
Music by Josip Slavenski
Première: April 22, 1928

42
POEMS OF 1917
Music by Leo Ornstein
Première: April 22, 1928

43
FRAGMENTS
Music by Louis Horst
Première: April 22, 1928

44
RESONANCES
Music by Gian Francesco Malipiero
Première: April 22, 1928

45
DANCE
Music by Arthur Honegger
Première: January 20, 1929

46
THREE FLORENTINE VERSES
Music by Domenico Zipoli
Première: January 20, 1929

47
FOUR INSINCERITIES
Music by Sergei Prokofieff
Première: January 20, 1929

48
CHANTS MAGICS
Music by Frederico Mompou
Première: January 20, 1929

49
TWO VARIATIONS
Music by Alexander Gretchaninoff
Première: January 20, 1929

50
UNBALANCED
Music by Tibor Harsányi
Première: March 3, 1929

51
ADOLESCENCE
Music by Paul Hindemith
Première: March 3, 1929

52
DANZA
Music by Darius Milhaud
Première: March 3, 1929

53
VISION OF THE APOCALYPSE
Music by Hermann Reutter
Première: April 14, 1929

54
MOMENT RUSTICA
Music by Francis Poulenc
Première: April 14, 1929

55
HERETIC
Old Breton Song
Première: April 14, 1929

56
SKETCHES FROM THE PEOPLE
Music by Julien Krein
Première: April 14, 1929

57
PRELUDE TO A DANCE
Music by Arthur Honegger
Première: January 8, 1930

58
TWO CHANTS
Music by Ernst Krenek
Première: January 8, 1930

59
LAMENTATION
Music by Zoltán Kodály
Première: January 8, 1930

60
**PROJECT IN MOVEMENT
FOR A DIVINE COMEDY**
Première: January 8, 1930

61
HARLEQUINADE
Music by Ernst Toch
Première: January 8, 1930

62
TWO PRIMITIVE CANTICLES
Music by Heitor Villa-Lobos
Première: February 2, 1931

63
PRIMITIVE MYSTERIES
Music by Louis Horst
Première: February 2, 1931

64
RHAPSODICS
Music by Béla Bartók
Première: February 2, 1931

65
BACCHANALE
Music by Wallingford Riegger
Première: February 2, 1931

66
DOLOROSA
Music by Heitor Villa-Lobos
Première: February 2, 1931

67
DITHYRAMBIC
Music by Aaron Copland
Première: December 6, 1931

68
SERENADE
Music by Arnold Schoenberg
Première: December 6, 1931

69
INCANTATION
Music by Heitor Villa-Lobos
Première: December 6, 1931

70
CEREMONIALS
Music by Lehman Engel
Première: February 28, 1932

71
OFFERING
Music by Heitor Villa-Lobos
Première: June 2, 1932

72
SALUTATION
Music by Carlos Chávez
Première: November 20, 1932

73
DANCE SONGS
Music by Imre Weisshaus
Première: November 20, 1932

74
CHORUS OF YOUTH
Music by Louis Horst
Première: November 20, 1932

75
ELEGIAC
Music by Paul Hindemith
Première: May 4, 1933

76
EKSTASIS
Music by Lehman Engel
Première: May 4, 1933

77
TRAGIC PATTERNS
Music by Louis Horst
Première: May 4, 1933

78
DANCE PRELUDE
Music by Nikolai Lopatnikov
Première: November 19, 1933

79
FRENETIC RHYTHMS
Music by Wallingford Riegger
Première: November 19, 1933

80
TRANSITIONS
Music by Lehman Engel
Première: February 18, 1934

81
PHANTASY
Music by Arnold Schoenberg
Première: February 18, 1934

82
FOUR CASUAL DEVELOPMENTS
Music by Henry Cowell
Première: February 18, 1934

83
CELEBRATION
Music by Louis Horst
Première: February 18, 1934

84
INTEGRALES
Music by Edgar Varèse
Première: April 22, 1934

85
DANCE IN FOUR PARTS
Music by George Antheil
Première: November 11, 1934

86
AMERICAN PROVINCIALS
Music by Louis Horst
Première: November 11, 1934

87
PRAELUDIUM
Music by Paul Nordoff
Première: February 10, 1935

88
COURSE
Music by George Antheil
Première: February 10, 1935

89
FRONTIER
Music by Louis Horst
Settings by Isamu Noguchi
Première: April 28, 1935

90
MARCHING SONG
Music by Lehman Engel
Première: April 28, 1935

91
PANORAMA
Music by Norman Lloyd
Settings by Arch Lauterer
Première: August 14, 1935

92
FORMAL DANCE
Music by David Diamond
Première: November 10, 1935

93
IMPERIAL GESTURE
Music by Lehman Engel
Première: November 10, 1935

94
HORIZONS
Music by Louis Horst
Settings by Alexander Calder
Première: February 23, 1936

95
CHRONICLE
Music by Wallingford Riegger
Settings by Isamu Noguchi
Première: December 20, 1936

96
OPENING DANCE
Music by Norman Lloyd
Première: July 30, 1937

97
IMMEDIATE TRAGEDY
Music by Henry Cowell
Première: July 30, 1937

98
DEEP SONG
Music by Henry Cowell
Première: December 19, 1937

99
AMERICAN LYRIC
Music by Alex North
Première: December 26, 1937

100
AMERICAN DOCUMENT
Music by Ray Green
Costumes by Edythe Gilford
Première: August 6, 1938

101
COLUMBIAD
Music by Louis Horst
Settings by Philip Stapp
Costumes by Edythe Gilfond
Première: December 27, 1939

102
"EVERY SOUL IS A CIRCUS"
Music by Paul Nordoff
Settings by Philip Stapp
Costumes by Edythe Gilfond
Première: December 27, 1939

103
EL PENITENTE
Music by Louis Horst
Settings by Arch Lauterer
Costumes by Edythe Gilfond
Première: August 11, 1940

104
LETTER TO THE WORLD
Music by Hunter Johnson
Settings by Arch Lauterer
Costumes by Edythe Gilfond
Première: August 11, 1940

105
PUNCH AND THE JUDY
Music by Robert McBride
Settings by Arch Lauterer
Costumes by Charlotte Trowbridge
Première: August 10, 1941

106
SALEM SHORE
Music by Paul Nordoff
Settings by Arch Lauterer
Costumes by Edythe Gilfond
Première: December 26, 1943

107
DEATHS AND ENTRANCES
Music by Hunter Johnson
Settings by Arch Lauterer
Costumes by Edythe Gilfond
Première: July 18, 1943

108
APPALACHIAN SPRING
Music by Aaron Copland
Settings by Isamu Noguchi
Costumes by Edythe Gilfond
Première: October 30, 1944

109
HERODIADE *(Mirror Before Me)*
Music by Paul Hindemith
Settings by Isamu Noguchi
Costumes by Edythe Gilfond
Première: October 30, 1944

110
IMAGINED WING
Music by Darius Milhaud
Settings by Isamu Noguchi
Costumes by Edythe Gilfond
Première: October 30, 1944

111
DARK MEADOW
Music by Carlos Chávez
Settings by Isamu Noguchi
Costumes by Edythe Gilfond
Première: January 23, 1946

112
CAVE OF THE HEART
(Serpent Heart)
Music by Samuel Barber
Settings by Isamu Noguchi
Costumes by Edythe Gilfond
Première: May 10, 1946

113
ERRAND INTO THE MAZE
Music by Gian Carlo Menotti
Settings by Isamu Noguchi
Première: February 28, 1947

114
NIGHT JOURNEY
Music by William Schuman
Settings by Isamu Noguchi
Première: May 3, 1947

115
DIVERSION OF ANGELS
(originally titled
(Wilderness Stair)
Music by Norman Dello Joio
Settings by Isamu Noguchi
Costumes with Oliver Gray
Première: August 13, 1948

116
JUDITH
Music by William Schuman
Settings by Charles Hyman, William
Sherman, Isamu Noguchi
Première: January 4, 1950

117
EYE OF ANGUISH
Music by Vincent Persichetti
Settings by Henry Kurth
Costumes by Fred Cunning
Première: January 22, 1950

118
GOSPEL OF EVE
Music by Paul Nordoff
Settings by Oliver Smith
Costumes by Miles White
Première: January 23, 1950

119
THE TRIUMPH OF SAINT JOAN
Music by Norman Dello Joio
Settings by Frederick Kiesler
Première: December 5, 1951

120
**CANTICLE FOR
INNOCENT COMEDIANS**
Music by Thomas Ribbink
Settings by Frederick Kiesler
Première: April 22, 1952

121
VOYAGE *
Music by William Schuman
Settings by Isamu Noguchi
Costumes by Edythe Gilfond
Première: May 17, 1953

Diversion of Angels: Linda Hodes, Mary Hinkson, and Helen McGehee and Company

*(new version THEATRE FOR A VOYAGE—May 5, 1955)

LeRoy Leatherman, a Louisianian, was educated at Vanderbilt University, Kenyon College, the University of Illinois, and Southern Methodist University. Novelist, short story writer, he first saw Martha Graham and her company perform in Dallas, Texas, in 1949, and he wrote about her first in 1950, when he served as company manager for her first appearances in Europe. In 1953 he became her personal manager and the director of her School. In 1961, after a year in France, he began writing and directing documentary films. He lives now in New York City, where he works with the Martha Graham Foundation and is writing his fourth novel.

Martha Swope was born in Texas and educated at Baylor University. In the mid 1950's she came to New York City and attended the School of American Ballet with the intention of making dancing a career. While in classes there, she met Jerome Robbins, who asked her to take some photographs of *West Side Story*. Her first published picture was one from this series, which appeared in *Life*. The same year Lincoln Kirstein asked her to become official photographer for the New York City Ballet Company, a position Miss Swope still holds. She photographed Miss Graham when the latter appeared in *Episode*s at the City Center with the New York City Ballet. Miss Graham was so pleased with her work that in 1960 Miss Swope became her official photographer.

The text of this book has been set in Linotype Trade Gothic
Light, an original design by Jackson Burke, executed by George
Ostrochulski in 1962. Display type has been set in Foundry
Trade Gothic Light and Standard. The paper is Superfine Text.
and the binding material is Lynnene.
The book was composed by Howard O. Bullard, Inc., New York,
and printed in Futuratone by Kingsport Press, Inc., Kingsport,
Tenn. Typography and binding design by Karl Leabo.